First World War
and Army of Occupation
War Diary
France, Belgium and Germany

16 DIVISION
48 Infantry Brigade
Royal Munster Fusiliers
1st Battalion
1 March 1916 - 31 October 1916

WO95/1975/3

The Naval & Military Press Ltd
www.nmarchive.com
Published in association with The National Archives

Published by

The Naval & Military Press Ltd

Unit 10 Ridgewood Industrial Park,

Uckfield, East Sussex,

TN22 5QE England

Tel: +44 (0) 1825 749494

www.naval-military-press.com

www.nmarchive.com

This diary has been reprinted in facsimile from the original. Any imperfections are inevitably reproduced and the quality may fall short of modern type and cartographic standards.

© **Crown Copyright**
Images reproduced by permission of The National Archives, London, England, 2015.

Contents

Document type	Place/Title	Date From	Date To
Heading	1975/3 1916 Mar-Oct 1 Battalion Royal Munster Fusiliers		
Heading	16th Division 48th Infy Bde 1st Bn Roy. Munster Fus 1916 Mar-Oct 1916 From Dardanelles 29 Div 86 Bde To 47 Bde 16 Div		
Heading	29th Division 86th Infantry Brigade Arrived Marseilles from Egypt 22nd March 1916 1st Battalion Royal Munster Fusiliers March 1916		
War Diary	Crewe Post - (Sinai Peninsula)	01/03/1916	02/03/1916
War Diary	El Kubri	03/03/1916	03/03/1916
War Diary	Suez	04/03/1916	14/03/1916
War Diary	H.T. Alaunia	15/03/1916	22/03/1916
War Diary	France	23/03/1916	23/03/1916
War Diary	Pont Remy	24/03/1916	24/03/1916
War Diary	Maison Roland	25/03/1916	31/03/1916
Miscellaneous	Appendix A	13/03/1916	13/03/1916
Miscellaneous	2nd Flight 29th Division Allotment Of Berthing Accommodation Appendix A		
Heading	29th Division 86th Infantry Brigade. G.H.Q. from 29th April 1916. Transferred to G.H.Q. 29th April 1916 1st Battalion Royal Munster Fusiliers April 1916 Operation Order Attached.	29/04/1916	29/04/1916
War Diary	Beauval	01/04/1916	04/04/1916
War Diary	Beaussart	05/04/1916	13/04/1916
War Diary	Trenches (Q 17 C.4.4. to Q 16 b. 6.4.)	13/04/1916	17/04/1916
War Diary	Trenches	18/10/1916	18/10/1916
War Diary	Mailly-Maillet	19/04/1916	23/04/1916
War Diary	Trenches	24/04/1916	24/04/1916
War Diary	Mailly-Maillet Line Of March Doulens	25/04/1916	25/04/1916
War Diary	Boulogne	26/04/1916	30/04/1916
Operation(al) Order(s)	86th Brigade Operation Order No. 44 Appendix A	02/04/1916	02/04/1916
Miscellaneous	March Table "A"		
Miscellaneous	Operation Order April 12th, 1916 Appendix B	12/04/1916	12/04/1916
Operation(al) Order(s)	86th Infantry Brigade Operation Order No. 45 Appendix Apr. B	11/04/1916	11/04/1916
Miscellaneous	March Table A.12/13th		
Miscellaneous	March Table "B" 13/14		
Miscellaneous	Field Cookers and all interchangeable stores should be arranged by brigades to be bended over to relieving Battalion on the 12th and 25th April.	12/04/1916	12/04/1916
Operation(al) Order(s)	86th Brigade Operation Order No. 46 Appendix Apr. C	17/04/1916	17/04/1916
Miscellaneous	Operation Orders April 23rd, 1916. By Lieut-Col. H.H. Monck-Mason, Comdg. 1st. Royal Munster Fusiliers.	23/04/1916	23/04/1916
Miscellaneous	Operation Orders April 24th, 1916	24/04/1916	24/04/1916
Operation(al) Order(s)	Operation Orders April 25th, 1916	25/04/1916	25/04/1916
War Diary	Boulogne	01/05/1916	28/05/1916
War Diary	Mazingarbe	29/05/1916	01/06/1916
War Diary	Philosophe East (Billets)	02/06/1916	02/06/1916
War Diary	Philosophe East	03/06/1917	05/06/1917
War Diary	Loos Section Left Sub Section Trenches	06/06/1916	08/06/1916

War Diary	Loos Section	09/06/1916	10/06/1916
War Diary	Village Lines	11/06/1916	13/06/1916
War Diary	Loos (Left Subsector)	14/06/1916	17/06/1916
War Diary	Mazingarbe	18/06/1916	26/06/1916
War Diary	Puit 14 Bis (Left Subsector)	27/06/1916	29/06/1916
War Diary	Tenth Avenue	30/06/1916	30/06/1916
Heading	War Diary 10th Battalion Royal Munster Fusiliers 1st. July To 31st. July 1916. Volume No.		
War Diary	10th Avenue 14 Bis Sect	01/07/1916	03/07/1916
War Diary	Right Sub Sect 14 Bis Sect	05/07/1916	07/07/1916
War Diary	Philosophe	08/07/1916	11/07/1916
War Diary	Noeux Les Mines	18/07/1916	19/07/1916
War Diary	Left Sub Sect Loos Sect.	22/07/1916	22/07/1916
War Diary	Mazingarbe	24/07/1916	24/07/1916
War Diary	Centre Sub Sect Hulluch Sect	27/07/1916	28/07/1916
Miscellaneous	48th Bde. No. S.L.S/G. 50 Appendix A	02/07/1916	02/07/1916
Miscellaneous	Equipment of above parties is given in the Appendix 4		
Miscellaneous	Situation Report Appendix B	07/07/1916	07/07/1916
Miscellaneous	Report On Attempted Enemy Raid Appendix B	07/07/1916	07/07/1916
Map Miscellaneous			
Miscellaneous	Report On New Crater Appendix C	27/07/1916	27/07/1916
Miscellaneous	Report On Operation On The Night Of 27-28 July 1916 Appendix D	27/07/1916	27/07/1916
Miscellaneous	Daily Strength and Casualties for July 1916 Appendix E		
Heading	War Diary 1st Royal Munster Fusiliers Month Of August, 1916 Volume		
War Diary	Right Sub Sect Hulluch	01/08/1916	08/08/1916
War Diary	Philosophe W.	12/08/1916	12/08/1916
War Diary	Left Sub Sect Hulluch	16/08/1916	16/08/1916
War Diary	Tenth Avenue	20/08/1916	20/08/1916
War Diary	Left Sub Hulluch	24/08/1916	24/08/1916
War Diary	Philosophe	25/08/1916	25/08/1916
War Diary	Allouagne	29/08/1916	29/08/1916
War Diary	Longueau	30/08/1916	30/08/1916
War Diary	Corbie	31/08/1916	31/08/1916
Miscellaneous	Appendix B	07/08/1916	07/08/1916
Operation(al) Order(s)	Operation Order 24 By Lieut Col. R.H. Monck-Mason, Comdg 1st Royal Munster Fusiliers Appendix C	07/08/1916	07/08/1916
Miscellaneous	Report On Operations On The Night Of The 20th. 21st Aug. 1916 Appendix G	21/08/1916	21/08/1916
Operation(al) Order(s)	Operation Orders No. 28 Appendix J	24/08/1916	24/08/1916
Miscellaneous	Casualties For August 1916	01/08/1916	01/08/1916
Heading	War Diary 1st Royal Munster Fusiliers For Month Of September, 1916 Volume		
War Diary	Sand Pit	01/09/1916	02/09/1916
War Diary	S.W. Billion Farm	03/09/1916	03/09/1916
War Diary	Bernafay Wood	04/09/1916	04/09/1916
War Diary	Trenches Facing Monchy	05/09/1916	05/09/1916
War Diary	In The Trenches S of Ginchy	06/09/1916	07/09/1916
War Diary	B.M.H.Q. Chalk Pit Guillemont Battalion In The Trenches	08/09/1916	08/09/1916
War Diary	Ginchy	09/09/1916	09/09/1916
War Diary	Happy Valley	10/09/1916	10/09/1916
War Diary	Corby	11/09/1916	17/09/1916
War Diary	Longpre	18/09/1916	20/09/1916

War Diary	Victoria Camp Westoutre	21/09/1916	23/09/1916
War Diary	Butterfly Farm	24/09/1916	26/09/1916
War Diary	Rossignol	27/09/1916	30/09/1916
Operation(al) Order(s)	Operation Order No. 31 By Lieut-col. R.H. Monck-Manson, Comdg. 1st Royal Munster Fus. Appendix A	02/09/1916	02/09/1916
Miscellaneous	Report On The Part Taken By The 1st Royal Minister Fusiliers On The Capture Of Ginchy Appendix B		
Operation(al) Order(s)	48th Infantry Brigade Operation Order No. 64. Appendix C	08/09/1916	08/09/1916
Operation(al) Order(s)	Operation Order No. 31A. Appendix D	08/09/1916	08/09/1916
Miscellaneous	Operation Order No.		
Operation(al) Order(s)	Operation Order No. 32. By Lieut-col. R.H. Monck-Mason, Comdg, 1st. Royal Munster Fusiliers Appendix E	11/09/1916	11/09/1916
Operation(al) Order(s)	Operation Order No. 33. By Lieut-Col R.H. Monck-Mason, Comdg. 1st. Royal Munster Fusiliers. Appendix F	17/09/1916	17/09/1916
Operation(al) Order(s)	Operation Order No. 34. By Lieut-Col R.H. Monck-Mason, Comdg. 1st. Royal Munster Fusiliers. Appendix G	20/09/1916	20/09/1916
Operation(al) Order(s)	Operation Order No. 35. By Lieut Col R.H. Monck-Mason, Comdg. 1st Royal Munster Fusiliers Appendix H	23/09/1916	23/09/1916
Operation(al) Order(s)	Operation Order No. 36 By Lieut Col. R.H. Monck-Mason, Comdg 1st R. Munster Fusiliers. Appendix I	27/09/1916	27/09/1916
Miscellaneous	Strength Diary. Appendix J	25/09/1916	25/09/1916
Heading	War Diary Month Of October, 1916 1st Munster Fusiliers Volume 8		
War Diary	In The Trenches	01/10/1916	04/10/1916
War Diary	Klondyke Farm	05/10/1916	20/10/1916
War Diary	Locre	21/10/1916	28/10/1916
War Diary	In The Trenches	29/10/1916	31/10/1916
Operation(al) Order(s)	Operation Order No. 37 By Lieut-Col. R.H. Monck-Mason. Comdg. 1st. Royal Munster Fusiliers Appendix B	30/09/1916	30/09/1916
Miscellaneous	Strength Oct. 27th		
Operation(al) Order(s)	Operation Order No. 38. By Lieut-Col. R.H. Monck-Mason, Comdg. 1st. Royal Munster Fusiliers Appendix C	01/10/1916	01/10/1916
Operation(al) Order(s)	Operation Order No. 39 By Lieut-Col. R.H Monck-Mason, Comdg. 1st R. Munster Fusiliers. Appendix D	04/10/1916	04/10/1916
Operation(al) Order(s)	Operation Order No. 40 By Lieut-Col. A.W. D.S.O., Comdg. 1st R. Munster Fusiliers. Appendix E	12/10/1916	12/10/1916
Operation(al) Order(s)	Operation Order No. 41 By Lieut-Col A.W. Clerke D.S.O. Comdg. 1st R. Munster Fus. Appendix F	21/10/1916	21/10/1916
Operation(al) Order(s)	Operation Order No. 42 By Lieut Col A.W. Clerke D.S.O. Comdg 1st R. Munster Fus. Appendix I	28/10/1916	28/10/1916

1975/3

1916 Mar - Oct

1 Battalion Royal Munster Fusiliers

16TH DIVISION
48TH INFY BDE

1ST BN ROY. MUNSTER FUS
MAY – OCT 1916

~~From Egypt~~

From Dardanelles 29 Div 86 BDE Box 4310

To 48 BDE 16 DIV

Box 1975

29th Division.
86th Infantry Brigade.

ARRIVED MARSEILLES FROM EGYPT 22nd March 1916.

1st BATTALION

ROYAL MUNSTER FUSILIERS.

MARCH 1916

BEF 86/29

Army Form C. 2118.

WAR DIARY
or
INTELLIGENCE SUMMARY
(Erase heading not required.)

1st Bn. Munster Fusiliers

March 1916

Hour, Date, Place	Summary of Events and Information	Remarks and references to Appendices

CREWE POST – 1st March
(SINAI PENINSULA)
    — 2 "
    — 3 "

2/Lt W. Fry Q.M. evacuated
28.01 from ALEXANDRIA joined details at EL KUBRI
Bn. H.Q. marched to EL KUBRI being relieved by 2/3rd Sikh Pioneers. Batt. strength off. 19 O.R. 252
at 15.30. Bad sand storm from the South the whole day.
Lt. Swipson & 1/Lt. Provis proceeded on sick leave to M.L.O. Victoria.

EL KUBRI – 3rd " — 07.00 Batt. crossed the Canal & marched to old camp in morning. SUEZ Batt.streng.off.18 o.r. 252
Lt. Musgrave Conson Relsin/Mr. Bouty reported for duty
  " Duffey & 19 o.r. joined 86th Bde. M.G. Coy. (Offr. from 4/3/16)
" Bowman & 26 o.r. (draughtsmen?) proceeded to Divisional Base at Ball.

SUEZ — 4 " —
  " — 5 " —
  " — 6 " —
  " — 7 " —
  " — 8 " —
  " — 11 " —
  " — 13 " —
  " — 14 " —

Capt. J.C.R. Williams from leave Lt. Chesney & 7 o.r. from Hosp. Batt. streng.off. 23 o.r. 252
Lt. Holt & 2 o.r. from ISMAILIA   " 24 " 252
Van de Wiele Departed 86th Bde. Bty & Ma. Chrimes from STAFF   " 25 " 261
28 o.r. returned to duty from ALEXANDRIA   " 25 " 210
    " 25 " 261
Divisional exchange at BIR SUEZ.
86th Bde. M.G.Coy. Embarked at SUEZ. Lt. Bowhurst on board (Cpl) reviewed
  05.30 Baggage left camp 08.30 Men to 86th Bde & staff   Batt. streng. off. 25 o.r. 287
  08.30 Batt. marched off. SUEZ docks 10.00. Embarked or (includes 4 o.r. att.)
  11.30 H.T."ALAUNIA" – Sailed 16.30 – Entered Canal 18.30

H.T."ALAUNIA" 15 " —
  " — 16 " —
  " — 22 " —

  09.00 Arr. PORT SAID – coaled here
  08.00 Sailed from PORT SAID
  10.00 Arr. MARSEILLES Batt. disembarked 11.30. Entrained at ARENC with Bgt. Stn. off. 24 o.r. 287
2 R.F. & 1 de Co. (at 14.56 of (2/4) (1 off. & 2 o.r. H.Q.Coy. at MARSEILLES)
Rau. DIJON MARSEILLES – Arr. ORANGE 23.00. Detrained & returned to troops

16.24

WAR DIARY / INTELLIGENCE SUMMARY

Army Form C. 2118.

13th Bn. Munster Fusiliers
March 1916

Port of March

Place	Date	Hour	Summary of Events and Information	Remarks and references to Appendices
FRANCE	22nd March	10.00	Arr. MARSEILLES. Batt. disembarked 11.30. Ex. Genl. Officer whilst 2 R. Fus. & details (Vide App 35 p 124)	Ref App sheet App 24 p. 287
		16.24	Train left MARSEILLES. Arr. ORANGE 23.00 – Tea & drinks for troops	
	23	10.10	Train arr. MACON. Tea provided – arr. LES LAUMES 21.00	
PONT REMY	24th	16.45	Detrained & marched to MAISON ROLAND – in billets. Arr. there by 21.00	App 25 p 325
			Batt. strength of 4th 38 offs. & above. There	
MAISON ROLAND	25th		Lt Sampson reports for duty from MARSEILLES	App 26 p. 325
	27F		Capt. C.R. Williams fell over the district of Pth day to Spmart. – Pph 2nd in march	" 26 " 325
	30th	12.00	Debus arrive & proceed into billets at CANDAS & BEAUVAL. Batt. billeting party left to RaM.	Appendix B
			Sampson 2 2nd Lts. proceeded to BEAUVAL – scheme of advance made to the Batt.	
			at the rate of 2 men per day B.U.K.	
	31st	09.15	Batt. left MAISON ROLAND. Tpts. arrested at LONGVILLERS at 10.30 & march 257	Batt Strength March 1st p. 24 p. 324
			BEAUMETZ – BERNAVILLE – FIENVILLERS – CANDAS & BEAUVAL. There was a 2	
			hour halt for dinner W. of FIENVILLERS at 13.00	
		17.30	All men in billets at BEAUVAL	

Appendix A

Secret

To Headqrs.
~~FFth Bte.~~
O.C. ~~2 Royal Fus.~~
1/R Munster Fus.
~~W Kent Field Coy RE~~
~~16th Sanitary Section~~

1. Orders have been received for the following troops, to embark on H.T. Alaunia (2nd Flight) at Suez on the 14th March.

    Second Flight
    2nd Royal Fusiliers
    1st R. Munster Fus.
    Chaplain
    West Kent Field Coy.
    Newfoundland Regt Battn.
    1/5th Royal Scots.
    ~~16th Sanitary Section~~ (if accommodation available).

2. Allotments of berthing accommodation are attached.

3. Duplicate nominal rolls and embarkation returns will be handed to the OC. NFLD Regt. by 0730. tomorrow.

4. The O.C. NFLD Regt. will detail a Ship's Adjutant, Ship's Sergt. Major, Q.master Sergt. and 8 other ranks, all of whom will report at the Embarkation Office Suez Docks at 0930 tomorrow with the nominal rolls and embarkation returns mentioned above.

5. Troops will be at Suez Docks at the following hours:-

    2nd Royal Fusiliers at 1100.
    West Kent Field Coy. 1130.
    1/R Munster Fus. 1200.
    Newfoundland Regt. 1245.
    1/5th R. Scots. 1330.
    ~~16th Sanitary Section~~ 1400.

6. Lunch will be provided for officers at 1300 on board ship. Tea will be the first meal for the troops, at 1600. The troops should therefore have their dinner before marching off.

7. Units will arrange direct with OC Train for necessary transport. Baggage must be at Suez Docks by 0900.

D.?.Key
Capt GS
29th Division

13/3/16.

2ND FLIGHT 29th Division.

Appendix A.
BR 15584/910
Table No. 9.

ALLOTMENT OF BERTHING ACCOMMODATION -

hely

H.T. ALAUNIA.

Unit	Officers	Other Ranks
Maximum Accommodation	200	1800.
2nd Royal Fusiliers	29	906.
1st R. Munster Fus.	24 25	290. 289
Chaplain.	1	-
West Kent Field Company.	5	153.
Newfoundland Battalion	25	577.
1/5th R. Scots.	26	301
~~1st Sanitary Section~~	~~5~~	~~27~~
	110	22~~27~~

29th Division.

86th Infantry Brigade.
8-------
G.H.Q. from 29th April 1916.

Transferred to G.H.Q. 29th April 1916.

1st BATTALION

ROYAL MUNSTER FUSILIERS

APRIL 1916

Operation Orders attached.

WAR DIARY or INTELLIGENCE SUMMARY

Army Form C. 2118.

1st Battn. B.E. Munster Fusiliers
April 1916 Vol I BEF

Hour, Date, Place	Summary of Events and Information	Remarks and references to Appendices
BEAUVAL 1st April	Capt. J.S. Omlinson apptd. & instructions S.O.H. FLIXECOURT	
" 2nd "	Orders received for Bde. to move into Divisional Reserve Area	Appendix Ap. A
" 3rd "	Batt. Wiltshires paraded to BEAUSSART Batt. Strth # Off 21 Or. 285	
" 4th " 09.00	Batt. left BEAUVAL. Brigade formed up E. of the tower at 09.30 & marched by BEAUQUESNE, MARIEUX, LOUVENCOURT & ACHEUX	
	Batt. followed by FORCEVILLE to BEAUSSART	
"	13.00 "A" Echelon left to Divine W. of VAUCHELLES	
BEAUSSART "	19.30 All men in billets – Battn. of Buckn. L.I. marched in at 18.30	
" 6 "	Batt. Strngth marching in # 20 Or. 280	
" " 16.00	O.C. & C./S.M. K.O.S.B. Trenches. Area shelled & trenches held by S.W.B. & Border Regt. were heavily shelled – Batt. Strngth # 17 Or. 271	
" " 21.00 & 22.45		
" 7 " 15.00	Batt. left VALNEUREUX for Colincamps	
" 8 " 10.30	Schoot at Colincamps & Bertrancourt Funds Mortar Considerable aerial activity on both sides	Batt. Strngth # 16 Or. 274 # 15 Or. 275
" 9 " 10.00	Major N.S. Malcolm proceeded to attend Senr. Officers course (4 weeks) at IV Army School at FLIXECOURT	# 22 Or. 274
" 10 "	A draft of 194 N.C.Os. & men reported for duty	(all ranks on leave are to be shown on the strngth)
" 11 "	Orders received for 86 – 87 – 88 & 88 – 87 in front Line trenches	Batt. Strngth Appendix Ap. B
" 13 " 15.30	Lawrence Porter of Battn. Mannads to take over from 1st Bn. Annandale Fusiliers in Frontline Trenches	# 21 Or. 497
" " 18.30	Remainder of Battn. proceeded to take over Area	M.f. Inspt FRANCE 57D S.5. 20000 # 17 C.4.4. & Q 16.4.6.4

Page 22

WAR DIARY / INTELLIGENCE SUMMARY

Army Form C. 2118.

1st Batt. Rl. Munster Fusiliers
April 1916

Hour, Date, Place	Summary of Events and Information	Remarks and references to Appendices
Trenches Q.17.c.4.4 & Q.16.b.6.4 — 13th April — 22:30	Relief by 2/Hants complete. Batt. rendezvous at Mr. Stiles were Established at ENGELBELMER	Batt. Strength Off. 22 O.R. 487
— 20:00 & 23:30	Enemy sent up 2 rains of coloured flares from the Q.17.b area Wigmans Farm	Batt. Strength Off. 21 O.R. 498 (at 26:00)
— 14th — 12:15	Aeroplane reported our line on left much damaged	Batt. Strength Off. 21 O.R. 494 Casualties 5 O.R. sick
14:00 to 15:00	Our trench gun shelled Enemy line in Q.17.b. Enemy artillery quiet all day	
— 15th —	Capt. W.L. de Ball & 2nd Lt. Smith reported for duty from 1st Reinf. Enemy artillery quiet all day — some snipers at Wigman's Farm	Batt. Strength Off. 21 O.R. 490 Casualties 5 O.R. sick
— 16th — 09:00 to 10:00	Enemy shelled our trenches intermittently. Maj. & Mrs. William & 2/Lieut Batt from FLIXECOURT	Batt. Strength 23 Off. 493 O.R. Casualties 1 O.R. wounded
— 20:00 & 23:00	Enemy M.G. Stoft our parapets 2 bays of our work heavily damaged. Rifle grenade & machine gun causing 5 casualties R/Os. Parties were withdrawn in ruined work after 20 minutes	
— 17th — 10:00 to 11:00	Enemy artillery fired on our trenches damaging wire at Q.18.4	Batt. Strength Off. 23 O.R. 487 Casualties 10 killed 4 wounded — 2 sick
— 13:00 & 17:30	Enemy artillery fired on our support trenches & support registered — orders received that the Batt. would be relieved by the 1st Batt. Lancaster Regt. & occupy billets at MAILLY MAILLET	Officer — Apr. C. [signature]

Page 23
Army Form C. 2118.

WAR DIARY
or
INTELLIGENCE SUMMARY

1st Batt. R. Munster Fusiliers
April 1916

(Erase heading not required.)

Hour, Date, Place	Summary of Events and Information	Remarks and references to Appendices
Trenches – 18 April – 12.00	Enemy artillery fired several rounds into our line.	Batt. Strength off 28 O.R. 481
– 19.00	Battn. was relieved by 2nd Batt. Lond. Rgt.	Casualties: O.R. wounded 3 –
– 23.30	Relief complete. Batt. went to billets at Mailly-Maillet.	Batt strength off 24 O.R. sickly 2.
MAILLY-MAILLET – 19th – 9.00	Batt. in billets. Lt. Col. Munster-Hazen arrived from the U.K.	Batt Strength off 22 O.R. 480
	& took over command of the Batt. from Major H.S. Wilson	Casualties: O.R. sick 1, O.R. killed 1
		[signature] Munster Fus.
MAILLY-MAILLET 18th April		
9.00	Capt & Temp Major H.S. Wilson took over the duties of Major in the H.Q. of Battalion.	
	Capt. C.H.D. Williams took over the duties of the Adjutant of the Corps	
	& Lieutenant reporting as 2nd Lieut. on duties	
	Strength of Battalion: Officers 26, O.R. 479. (Effective)	
MAILLY-MAILLET 20th April	In Billets.	
" 21st April	In Billets.	
	Capt B.H.S. Stephenson reported for duty from 4th BnRMF and took over command of X Coy.	
" 14.30	from 2nd Lieut Creasy. Battalion rose	
	Battalion proceeded to 5th Avenue for digging. 400 of Communication Trench were	
	broad wed. of states	
" 22 April 4.30	Battalion returned to Billets. Party were unmolested while work was in progress.	
	Lieut W.E. Molesworth reported for duty from 3rd Bn RMF.	
	Lieut H.H.Lake having been invalided to U.K. is struck off the strength of the Batt."	

Page 24

Army Form C. 2118.

1st Batt. R. Munster Fusiliers
April 1916

WAR DIARY
or
INTELLIGENCE SUMMARY

(Erase heading not required.)

Hour, Date, Place		Summary of Events and Information	Remarks and references to Appendices
MAILLY-MAILLET 23rd April		Batt received orders to relieve 1st Batt Lanc Fusiliers in the trenches. 1 Coy went from the reserve with orders of O.C. 1 R.M.F.	Appendix. Op. Ord. 1 RMF 2/23/4/16. A.1.
	10.30	O.C. proceeded to Trenches.	
	12.00	O.C. visited green Trenches from with Major Magniac Comdg 1st L.F.	
	19.30	Batt marched out in relief of 1st L.F.	
	21.30	Relief commenced	Batt Strength. Officers 26. o.r. 970
Trenches " 24th April 01.30		Relief completed and reported by telephone to G.O.C. 86th Brigade	Appendix Op. Ord. 1 RMF 2/24/4/16. A.2.
		Batt received orders that the RMF were to be temporarily withdrawn from the 29th Division and Transferred to lines of Communications at BOULOGNE Base, for the purpose of recruiting and Training, and would be relieved in the trenches to-night of 24th April by the following troops:— 2 Coy 1st 7. L.F., 1st R.Dub Fus.	
		G.S. relief battalion trenches from O.C. 1 RMF.	
	14.00	Relief commenced	
	20.00	All quiet in this part of the line.	
MAILLY-MAILLET 25th April 05.30		Relief completed and reported by telephone to G.O.C. 86th Brigade	Appendix Op. or. 1 RMF 2/25/4/16 A.8
Line of march	12.00	Battalion marched off from MAILLY MALLET en route for DOULENS. (about 15 Miles)	
DOULENS	19.30	Battalion arrived DOULENS.	Batt Strength. Officer 26. o.r. 470
"	22.35	" " entrained	Batt Strength Officer 26 o.r. 476
BOULOGNE 26th April 05.30		Battalion arrived BOULOGNE and detrained and marched to St MARTINS Camp	
" 27th April	10.00	Took over Barracks Rue de la Science. from 2nd Monmouthshire Reg.	
		The following detachments proceeded as follows:—	
	09.50	CALAIS. 2 Coy. 4 Officers v 170 o.r. (completed from W&Z Coy.) Gare Centrale. Major Wilson Lieut Ponylester 2 Lieut Cornish 2 Lieut Fisher.	
	09.54	AUDREUIQ v RCTSmith v RCTSmith 3 Sergts v 28 o.r. from Y Coy. Gare Centrale	Batt Strength Officer 26 o.r. 472

Page 25
Army Form C. 2118.

1st Batt R Munster Fusiliers
April 1916

WAR DIARY
or
INTELLIGENCE SUMMARY

(Erase heading not required.)

Hour, Date, Place	Summary of Events and Information	Remarks and references to Appendices
BOULOGNE 27th April (continued) 1632	DESVRES. 1 Sqt = g. or. M.G, Gre Centrale. MONTREUIL 1 Sgt = g. or. 2 G, gre Central. Lieut Creagy (g.M.) transferred to 86th Bde M.G. Coy to strike off the strength of the Battalion.	Strength Batt Offr 24 - O.R.s 568
" 28th April	Draft of 120 NCO & men reported Infantry from ROUEN	
" 29th April	Capt. B & S Stevenson proceeded t CALAIS to relieve Major HS Wilson	
" 30th April	nil.	
	nil	

S E C R E T.   Appendix to GA No.6.

86TH BRIGADE OPERATION ORDER NO.44

Ref. Map 1/60,000 Set B Sheet 12.   BEAUVAL,
                                                      2-4-16.

1. The Brigade will move into the Divisional Reserve Area on the 4th inst. in accordance with attached March Table "A".

2. Order of march as under:-

    Brigade Headquarters.
    Machine Gun Company
    Royal Munster Fusiliers.
    Royal Dublin Fusiliers.
    Lancashire Fusiliers.
    Royal Fusiliers.
    Kent Field Co., R.E.
    89th Field Ambulance. → Pass S.P. at 1000
    Train waggons.

3. Head of column to pass junction of BEAUVAL-DOULLENS Road and the Northerly BEAUVAL-BEAUQUESNE Road at 0930.

4. There will be an hour and 10 minutes halt for dinners; time notified en route.

5. One Officer per Battalion will be detailed to collect the stragglers of his Unit, and bring them on in a formed body.

    In addition one platoon of 2nd Royal Fusiliers will be detailed as rearguard to assist in this duty.

6. On reaching the vicinity of ACHEUX Units must be prepared to take military precautions if subjected to shell fire.

    Formed bodies of troops must not enter BEAUSSART and ENGLEBELMER until after dusk.

7. The Refilling Point on April 5th will be on ACHEUX-LEALVILLERS Road.

8. Orders re destination of transport of BEAUSSART and ENGLEBELMER Units to be given verbally.

                                                    Ian Grant.
                                                         Capt.,
Issued at, 1330   Brigade Major, 86th Bde.

Copy No. 1-2 War Diary   8. Bde Machine Gun Co.
         3   Office   9. Kent Field Co.RE.
         4   Royal Fus.   10. 89th Field Ambulance
         5   Lancashire Fus.   11. No.2 Co. A.S.C.
         6   R.Munster Fus.   12. 29 Div. (for information)
         7   R.Dublin Fus.

MARCH TABLE "A"

UNIT	FROM	TO	VIA	REMARKS.
86th Brigade Headquarters Brigade Machine GUN CO. R.Dublin Fusrs. Lancashire Fusrs. 89th Field Ambulance	BEAUVAL	ACHEUX	BEAUQUESNE MARIEUX LOUVENCOURT	
R.Munster Fusrs.	"	BEAUSSART	BEAUQUESNE MARIEUX LOUVENCOURT ACHEUX FORCEVILLE	Halting under cover until dusk on clearing ACHEUX if situation demands.
Royal Fusrs. Kent Field Co. R.E.	"	ENGLEBEL MER	BEAUQUESNE MARIEUX LOUVENCOURT ACHEUX FORCEVILLE MEDAUVILLE	Halting under cover if dusk on clearing ACHEUX if situation demands.

appendix Apr. 13

No. 3.   OPERATION ORDERS APRIL 12th, 1916.
:-:-:-:-: :-:-:-:-: -:-:-:-:-:-:-:-:-:-:-:-:-:-:-:-:

By Capt. C.R. Williams, Comdg. 1st. Royal Munster Fus.

(1) The Battalion will proceed to the trenches to-morrow night (13/14) to take over that part of the line at wresent held by the 1st. Royal Enniskilling Fusiliers. One company of the 2nd Royal Fusiliersw will be in reserve under the orders of O.C. 1st. R.M.F.

(2) W. Company will furnish a party of 3 N.C.O's and 18 men to take over a mine and listening galleries.
The regimental signallers under the senior N.C.O. will accompany this party which will parade at 10-15.

(3) The following parties will leave at 1330:-
Cook sergeant and 1 cook per company (to take over cookers).
1 N.C.O. and 2 pioneers to take over water and sanitary arrangements
Regimental Sergeant Major and 1 storeman and Bomb sergeant to take over stores, ammunition bombs etc., at Headquarter dump.
1 officer per company and 1 representative per platoon to take over trench stores.

(4) Companies will leave poesent billets at intervals of 15 minutes in the following order:- W. company
X. "
Y. "
Z. "
W. Company will leave at 1830 and take over the right of the line.
X company at 1845 and take over the left.
Y. and Z. companies will leave at 1900 and 1915 respectively and be in support.
Lewis Gun detachment will leave in their own time under 2/Lt. J.A. Addinsell. Guides will meet all these parties where the MAILLY MAILLET RD enters ENGELBELMER.

(5) Coy.Qr.Mr. Sgts will remain in ENGELBELMER and bring up rations to the Battalion.
The snipers and bombers will be attached to W. company for rations. The Lewis gunners to Y. company, the signallers, stretcher bearers and Headquarter details to Z company.

(6) Equipment will always be worn by all ranks when in the front line trench, with the exception of bombers on duty, who will wear bomb waistcoats.
Gas helmets must always be worn outside the great coat.
Dug outs in the front line will not be used by night

(7) All officers spare kits will be taken to the Quartermaster's stores by 1200 for removal to Battalion dump at ENGELBELMER.

Time issued:- 21-30

Copy No. 9   *[signature]*   Capt.
                                             a/Adjutant.

S E C R E T.   86TH INFANTRY BRIGADE OPERATION ORDER NO.45

Appendix / Copy No. 5

ACHEUX.
11-4-1916.

Ref. 57D S.E. Map.
1/20,000.

1. The Brigade will relieve the 87th Brigade in the front line on the nights of the 12/13 and 13/14th.

Reliefs as under:-

night of 12/13th. R.DUBLIN FUSILIERS relieve BORDER REGT."in toto"

ROYAL FUSILIERS relieve SOUTH WALES BORDERERS at MAILLY MAILLET and AUCHONVILLERS.

night of 13/14th. Brigade Headquarters relieve H.Qrs., 87th Bde.

Bde.Machine Gun Co.relieve Bde.Machine Co. 87th Bde "in toto"

LANCASHIRE FUSILIERS relieve K.O.S.B. "in toto".

R.MUNSTER FUSILIERS relieve R.INNISKILLING FUS. firing line and supports.

One Company ROYAL FUSILIERS relieves Reserve Company R.INNISKILLING FUSILIERS.

Under orders OC 1/R.M.F

2. The moves will be carried out in accordance with the attached March Tables "A" and "B".

3. Battalions will relieve a proportion of their specialists, machine gunners, telephonists, etc., and take over Company and Battalion trench stores by day.

4. Units will arrange direct with the Units they are relieving for the provision of trench guides for Companies or platoons rendezvous at which they are to meet etc.

5. The Field Ambulance have established Advanced Dressing Stations in RUE MONTIGNY, MAILLY MAILLET and in AUCHONVILLERS.

6. Units will report to Brigade H.Qrs. on completion of relief.

Issued at. 17.30.....

Captain,
Brigade Major, 86th Bde.

Copy No.1 and 2 War Diary.   Copy No .6 R.Dublin Fus.
  "   No.3 Royal Fusiliers.   "   No.7 Bde Machine Gun Co.
  "   No.4 Lancashire Fus.   "   No .8 No.2 Co., A.S.C.
  "   No.5 R.Munster Fusiliers.   "   No.9 87th Bde (for information)
                                        "   No.10 88th Bde (-"-)

MARCH TABLE 4. 12/13th.

Unit.	From	To	Via	Remarks.
ROY. DUB. FUS.	ACHEUX	Front Line	FORCEVILLE - ENGLEBELMER 1st AVENUE.	After 1815.
ROYAL FUSILIERS	ENGLEBELMER	MAILLY MAILLET ANCRE VALLEY.	Direct.	After 1830. Two Platoons in FORTE MOULIN and PRONEE on roller by 88th Bde.. The Battalion will continue to find mining fatigue until 15th inst..

Ref: 57 D.S.E. Map 1/20,000.

M A R C H — T A B L E. "B" 13/14.

Unit.	From	To.	via.	Remarks.
1st LANCS: FUSX	ACHEAUX	Front line	FORCEVILLE - MAILLY MAILLET AUCHONVILLERS.	After 1815.
86th BDE. H.Q's.	ACHEAUX	MAILLY MAILLET	3rd AVENUE - FORCEVILLE	
ROY. MUN. FUSRS:	BEUSSART	Front Line	MAILLY MAILLET CONSTITUTION HILL	After 1845
1 COY:ROYAL FUSRS:	MAILLY-MAILLET	Knightsbridge BARRACKS	~~FORCEVILLE~~	After 1900
BDE. MACHINE GUN COY:	ACHEAUX	MAILLY-MAILLET	FORCEVILLE	Follow 1st Lanc: Fusrs:.

HEADQUARTERS,
29th DIVISION.
No. A394/2

Field Cookers and all interchangeable stores should be arranged by brigades to relieving Battalions on the 12th and 18th April.

The following table will show how these exchanges can be effected.

	From		To	Interchange with	Date
86th Brigade	1 Bn.	Acheux	Front line	1 Bn. 87th Bde. at Front line	12th April.
	1 Bn.	Englebelmer	Mailly	1 Bn. 87th "	"
87th "	1 Bn.	Front line	Acheux	1 Bn. 86th " : " Acheux	" "
	1 Bn.	Mailly	Louvencourt	1 Bn. 86th " : " Louvencourt	" "
88th "	1 Bn.	Louvencourt	Englebelmer	1 Bn. 86th " " Englebelmer	" "
	1 Bn.	"	Mailly	Take their own Cookers &c.	" "
86th "	1 Bn.	Beaumont	Front line	1 Bn. 87th Bde. at Front line	18th "
	1 Bn.	Acheux	"	1 Bn. "	" "
87th "	1 Bn.	Front line	Acheux	1 Bn. 86th " : " Acheux	" "
	1 Bn.	"	Louvencourt	1 Bn. 86th " " Louvencourt	" "
88th "	1 Bn.	Louvencourt	Englebelmer	Take their own Cookers &c.	" "
	1 Bn.	"	Beaumont	1 Bn. 86th Bde.Beaumont	" "
	1 Bn.	Arqueves	Mailly	Take their own Cookers &c.	" "

11/4/16.

N. C. Ryan
Captain,
D.A.A. & Q.M.G. 29th Division.

Appendix Ap. C
Copy No 3

SECRET.

86TH BRIGADE OPERATION ORDER NO.46.

MAILLY-MAILLET.
17-4-16.

1. The 4th Battalion Worcester Regiment leave here, Mailly, at 1930, 19th inst., to take over that part of our line now held by 1st R.Munster Fusiliers and 1st R.Dublin Fusiliers from E.Street (Q 10.5) southwards.

2. The O.C., 4th Battalion Worcester Regiment, will communicate personally with O.C., 1st R.Munster Fusiliers over the relief, and the O.C's, 1st R.Dublin Fusiliers and 1st R.Munster Fusiliers will arrange for guides and meeting places.

3. On relief the 1st R.Munster Fusiliers will occupy billets in MAILLY. A billeting officer will be sent in first thing in the morning to take over billets.

4. The point of junction of the 1st Lancashire Fusiliers and 1st R.Dublin Fusiliers, after this relief, will be the new Beaumont Road, Q.4.4. Time of relief will be arranged by O.C's these Battalions.

5. The 1st R.Munster Fusiliers will hand over their gas cookers and tools in exchange for those which they will take over from the relieving Battalion. The 1st R.Dublin Fusiliers will hand over such proportion of trench stores as are now in that part of their line to be handed over.

6. Battalion Headquarters of 1st R.Dublin Fusiliers will be handed over to 88th Brigade on the 24th; another Battalion Headquarters will be prepared in the vicinity of AUCTION LODGE.

7. Those guns of the Machine Gun Co. now South of TIPPERARY AVENUE will be relieved by 88th Brigade during the course of the week; on relief the Machine Gun Company will take over gun positions from 88th Brigade in AUCHONVILLERS.

Issued at...2000...

Rott Lee Capt.,
Staff Captain, 86th Bde. *for Bde Major*

Copy No.1 War Diary.
    2 Office.
    3 1st R.Mun.Fus.
    4 2nd Royal Fus.
    5 1st R.Dublin Fus.

Copy No.6 1st Lancs.Fusrs.
    7 Machine Gun Co.
    8 4th Worcesters (for information
    9 86th Bde   -"-

No.5.

OPERATION ORDERS APRIL 23rd, 1916.

By Lieut-Col. R.H. Monck-Mason, Comdg. 1st. Royal Munster Fusiliers.

The Battaliion will proceed to the trenches to-night (23/24) to take over that part of the line at present held by the 1st. Lancashire Fus.
    One company Lancashire Fus. will be in reserve and under the orders of O.C. 1st. R.M.F.

(2)   The following parties will leave at 1330 and proceed by 5th Avenue at intervals.
    Cook sergeant and 1 cook per company to take over cookers.
    1 N.C.O. and 2 pioneero to take over water and sanitary arrangements
    A/R.S.M. and 1 storeman and bomb sergeant to take over stores, ammunition, bombs etc., at headquarter dump.
    1 officer per company and 1 representative per platoon to take over trench stores.
    Signalling sergeant and 4 signallers to take over lines of communication.
    Companies will leave present billets at times to be notified later.

(3)   O.C. companies will arrange to visit the trenches this morning and take over lines as follows:-
    W. Coy 1st. R.M.F. from A. Coy. 1st. Lancashire Fus.
    X. " "   "   " B. " 1st.   "   "
    Y. " "   "   "C. " 1st.   ".   "
    Z. " "   " D. " 1st.   "   "

(4)   Lewis gun detachment will leave under orders of Lt. D.P. Hall, they must be in the trenches by 1500.

(5)   Coy.Qr.Mr. Sgts will remain in Mailly and bring up rations to the Battalion.

(6)   All officers kits will be handed in at Quartermaster's stores by 1800.

                                              (signed) C.R. Williams,
                                                    Capt. & Adjutant.

OPERATION ORDERS APRIL 24th, 1916.

By Lieut-Col. R.H. Monck-Mason, Comsg. 1st. Royal Munster Fusiliers.

(1) The Battalion is being temporarily withdrawn from the Brigade and will be relieved in the trenches to-night.

(2) One company of Royal dublin Fusiliers, (200 other ranks) will take over the line from the left of W. coy. up to Sap 7, and a company of Lancashire Fus the remainder of the Front Line.
The Lancashire Fus. will relieve Z. Coy in the reserve line.

(3) O.C. Companies will report at Battalion Headquarters when their companies are relieved, and then march off independently to Mailly where they will be billeted to-night. They will arrange to enter Mailly by the road leading past the station where they will be met by guides and conducted to their billets.

(4) All trench stores are to be handed over including periscopes.

(5) The cook sergeant and 1 cook per company will proceed independently to Mailly.

(6) All blankets are to be carried.

(Signed) C.R. Williams, Capt.,

Adjutant.

No.7.

OPERATION ORDERS APRIL 25th, 1916.

By Lieut-Col. R.H. Monck-Mason, Comdg. 1st. Royal Munster Fusiliers.

(1) The Battalion will leave DOULLENS by train for Boulogne at 2128 to-day complete with 1st. Line Transport, arriving at Boulogne at 0348 on 26th inst.

(2) Companies and Transport will be ready to move off at 1100. Further details as to order of march will be issued later.

(3) All steel helmets will be handed in to the Quartermaster at the Brigade Dump at 0945.
2 Lewis Guns will be handed over to the 16th Middlesex Rgt. at 1030.
Telescopic rifles will be handed over to the Brigade Office at 1030.
Blankets are to be rolled and dumped on the side of the ACHEUX Rd at 1000.
2 Cookers will be drawn from the 16th Middlesex Rgt, 1 from the Royal Dublin Fusiliers and 1 from 1st. Lancashire Fusiliers.
Any periscopes, very pistolo trench boots or any trench stores and surplus S.A.A. in possession of tie Battalion will be handed in to the Quartermaster at the Brigade dump at 0945.

(4) All maps must be handed in to the Adjutant (in the hhuts) by 1100 without fail.

(signed) C.R. Williams, Capt.,

Adjutant.

WAR DIARY
or
INTELLIGENCE SUMMARY

Army Form C. 2118.

May 1916

Hour, Date, Place	Summary of Events and Information	Remarks and references to Appendices
BOULOGNE		

Army Form C. 2118.

WAR DIARY
or
INTELLIGENCE SUMMARY

(Erase heading not required.)

1st Royal Marine Bn

Instructions regarding War Diaries and Intelligence Summaries are contained in F. S. Regs., Part II. and the Staff Manual respectively. Title pages will be prepared in manuscript.

Hour, Date, Place	Summary of Events and Information	Remarks and references to Appendices
17th May BOULOGNE	2 Lieut. D.E. Green placed on Staff Liaison	
	Capt. J.C. Wilson reported off sick leave	
	Capt. B.H. Purdue — M. Batt from W.O. R.M?	
06.30	2 Lieut C.B. Callander report [in draft by 3rd Batt RMLI (RMO)]	
	W. Coy under Capt. Weyman left 1st line at Proceeded to CALAIS via boat	B.H. Strength 4th officers 30 — 556
	9 x Coy	
18th May BOULOGNE 17.30	X Coy under Capt. Stevenson 3 off + 104 ov reported arrival from CALAIS	
	on H. Reg. Capt. Pinker proceeded to RMR leave from CALAIS	
	2 in Com reported arrival officers	
19 May "	And	B.H. Strength 4 offs 30 + 1556
20 " "	And	
21 " "	CO: Lt. Anwyl Procyon on Staff leave from CALAIS	
	Capt. R.H. Brown reel. Exped. reported (ex. casualty from 4. Batt)	CH Strength 6 off + 31 + 682
22 " "	Steven rejoined that Batt will be relieved at manee de Soussie 9	
23 " "	1st N.Staff Queens Batt being opened to HASTING Camp on	
	relief.	
24 " " 19.00	W. Coy at ANDRUICG 508 marched and SWANTON in Oct	
	lt. Lighty Proceed y May Leave	
25 " "	Joined Detachment at Casandia under Lt Scorer	
	07.00 Batt Movement to Casandia	
	09.00 Bivouacs Erection	
	10.00 R. Col. Lampert	

RHP

WAR DIARY or INTELLIGENCE SUMMARY

(Erase heading not required.)

Army Form C. 2118.

Instructions regarding War Diaries and Intelligence Summaries are contained in F. S. Regs., Part II. and the Staff Manual respectively. Title pages will be prepared in manuscript.

Hour, Date, Place	Summary of Events and Information	Remarks and references to Appendices
BOULOGNE 25th Aug (arrived)	Batt. at ST MARTIN'S CAMP and pieced up kits for move by train	Batt. Strength Off. 31 OR. 680
26 Aug BOULOGNE	2nd Lt Brown reported and joined Batt.	
27 " "	Orders received that Batt. was moving from Boulogne on 28th May to join main Body — out from Base 9 to 16th Division	
28 Aug	20.00 12 Officers & advance party of Gun Corps	
	03.15 Batt. marched to STARTING point	
	04.00 Entrained for Corbie	
In train	03.35 Batt. left BOULOGNE & train in BETHUNE	
BETHUNE	11.00 Arrived at BETHUNE in motor	Special Batt. strength
Finginhem	13.00 Arrived and 3 BETHUNE & units in MAZINGARBE	Off. 31 OR 462
	15.30 8 O.C. 16 & O.R. in truck at NOEUX-LES-MINES	Off. 27 OR 635
MAZINGARBE	16.00 Batt. marched to off loc	
	18.00 Ration & CB.H. Reached the camp Ltd. 2nd Armies in Trench's posn ...	
	... (trenches)	
	H.Q. C.H. & C Coys relieved to BR in ... of Trenches of Hingingeh	
	H.Q. Coy. Ou & D detached. H.Q. of	
29 & 30 MAZINGARBE	Batt. in trenches	
30 Aug	2 off and Dy supplied groups for R of Bt Argunes from ...	Batt Strength Off. 30 OR 747
31 Aug	... 2nd Lt to ... join 10th THEOPHE Regt ...	
	Orders received that unit to move unit from Engr Resec on 2-9-16.	R. Mauro, Major Comdg 1st R.E. Batt.

Army Form C. 2118.

XVI

1st R Munster Fusiliers

Vol 5

WAR DIARY
or
INTELLIGENCE SUMMARY

(Erase heading not required.)

Instructions regarding War Diaries and Intelligence Summaries are contained in F.S. Regs., Part II. and the Staff Manual respectively. Title pages will be prepared in manuscript.

Hour, Date, Place	Summary of Events and Information	Remarks and references to Appendices
1916		
1st June MAZINGARBE	11 NCOs and Men reported for duty from 9th 13th R.Ir.F.	Batt Strength Offrs 38 o.r. 807
15.00	5 Stretchers were dropped in the vicinity of Hut Camp. Otherwise quiet.	
	6 Men reported for duty from the 16th Bn Cyclist Corps	
2nd June PHILOSOPHE EAST (Billets) 14.30	48 NCOs and Men reported for duty from 29th Div. Base Details ROUEN.	
15.00	Battalion marched out of MAZINGARBE arrived PHILOSOPHE EAST.	Batt Strength Offrs 38 o.r 950
17.00	Relief of 7th R.Munster Fusiliers completed.	
	All quiet nothing to report.	
3rd June PHILOSOPHE EAST.	2nd Lt C.J. Murphy reported for duty from 1 to 9th Bn R.M.Fus.	
17.30	Two shells of large calibre were dropped 3 near the Guardroom to N-East and N.0 where trolly crosses the road. Another at the end of road near junction of LENS road. One man dangerously wounded, three severely, and seven slightly.	Batt Strength Offrs 35 o.r. 995
	Otherwise quiet. Two of above men fit for duty.	
4th June PHILOSOPHE EAST	All quiet, nothing to report.	Batt Strength Offrs 35 o.r.1000
5th June PHILOSOPHE EAST	All quiet, nothing to report. 2nd Lieut J.G. Harold Berry, 2nd Lieut J.T. Murphy, 2nd Lt E.P. Conley reported for duty. The former from 5th O'Munsters the two latter from 4th Munsters arrived for duty.	Batt Strength Offrs 38 o.r. 1000
6th June LOOS Section Left Subsection Trenches 17.30	Batt marched out of PHILOSOPHE en route to relieve 7 RIR in trenches.	
22.00	Relief completed.	
23.30	Enemy working party digging at SEAFORTH CRATER were fired on by Lewis Guns but enemy continued working. W.Coy	

Army Form C. 2118.

1st R' Munster Fus II

WAR DIARY
or
INTELLIGENCE SUMMARY
(Erase heading not required.)

Instructions regarding War Diaries and Intelligence Summaries are contained in F. S. Regs., Part II. and the Staff Manual respectively. Title pages will be prepared in manuscript.

Hour, Date, Place	Summary of Events and Information	Remarks and references to Appendices
1916		
6th June (continued) 21.00 to 23.00	Enemy fired many rifle grenades, no damage done. (W.Coy. Capt Murray)	Batt. Strength of 41 o.r. 997
7th June LOOS Sector (as above) 02.00	Enemy working party found working all night opposite Gordon Alley, however guns were turned on them continually. Considerable sniping opposite CAMERON Alley & many tonight. Also 10 Rifle grenades were (mostly enemy opposite GORDON Alley) no damage done (Capt Pearse X Coy)	
12.45 03.00	Enemy rang between Firing line and support line, also Physquads were fired no damage was done. Enemy snipers on firing & support line snipers active. H.31.B.3.2.	
03.40	6 Lells HE shrapnel over a howitzer were men wounded.	
04.00	Enemy Rifle grenades active on firing line, no damage. Returned similar attention mostly on bob dug out. hand Coy Head quarters opposite SEAFORTH Crater intermittently. Enemy fired rifle grenades opposite SEAFORTH Crater intermittently all night.	
	Enemy fired during the day rifle grenades bombs in fairful between BLACKWATCH Alley and GORDON Alley & three places. Capt Murray W Coy intermittent withdrew the HE. a communication trench's junction of ENGLISH Alley and Support Trench. Snipers active. No casualties. Capt Pearse Y Coy	
20.30	W Coy opened fire on SEAFORTH CRATER and a trench right and left. rifle grenades. Enemy retaliated. W were silenced.	
22.30 & 23.15	Patrols were sent of Y Coy were reported into condition.	Batt. Strength of 41 o.r. 995
	Casualties 2 Lieut McCleugh slightly.	

III

Army Form C. 2118.

1st Royal Munster Fusiliers

WAR DIARY or INTELLIGENCE SUMMARY

(Erase heading not required.)

Hour, Date, Place	Summary of Events and Information	Remarks and references to Appendices
1916		
8th June LOOS Section 24.30 (Left Subsection)	Enemy working party could be heard at SEAFORTH CRATER. Remainder of night fairly quiet.	
08.30	Enemy who seemed to possess a GORDON Alley from a point N. of SEAFORTH Crater, we retaliated with rifle grenades. Enemy ceased.	Casualties 1 slight Batt Strength Offrs 41 ORs 995
23.30	Wiring party went out and returned un injured, report that wire at Collection appears from the Trenches as been ridden by long grass. Capt Punton X Coy. Co. Samhill slight	Casualties
9th June LOOS Section 6.30	Very little action on our front. We are of the left hand makers on N side of SEAFORTH Crater. Enemy retaliated with heavy mortar but no damage was done.	Casualties 2 men wounded slight Batt Strength 41 Offrs 990 OR
21.30	On Right of line our Rifle grenades were fairly active all day, then a few rifle grenades were fired by Enemy during the day, no damage done. Distance quiet. Enemy fired heavy rifle grenade fire on Right of line & SEAFORTH Crater, we retaliated and enemy ceased.	
23.30	Enemy working party in SEABORN Crater fired on.	
10th June LOOS Section 01.5	Officer patrol reconnoitred GREEN MOUND. found it unoccupied by enemy. About 25 tar barrels and 12 feet deep.	
	Remainder of Day Quiet. With exception of a few trench mortar shells fired at Cont Trench X Coy. No damage done.	Casualties 2 slightly wounded in Batt Strength 44 Off 983 OR
18.30	Relief by 1 R.I.R. Completed. Batt in VILLAGE LINES W Coy ENCLOSURE Right Sub section X Coy VILLAGE LINES Y Coy DUMP Street Z Coy ENCLOSURE.	
20.30	Relief of 9 R.D.W. in VILLAGE LINES Completed. Batt in Brigade Support.	
	Following officers joined: Rev J. E. Tumney from 9th R.M.F. 2 Lt Saunders from Lt Ball R.M.F. 2 Lt Hayman from 3rd Bn R.M.F.	
11th June VILLAGE LINES	Nothing to report	Batt Strength 43 Offs 983 OR Casualties 1 OR Reported missing wounded Batt belonging to Army in LOOS

Army Form C. 2118.

WAR DIARY
or
INTELLIGENCE SUMMARY
(Erase heading not required.)

1st Royal Munster Fusiliers

Hour, Date, Place	Summary of Events and Information	Remarks and references to Appendices
1916		
12th June VILLAGE LINES	Nothing to report	Batt Strength off 43 or 988
13 June "	Nothing to report	Batt Strength off 43 or 979
14th June LOOS (Left Subsector)	Batt moved down to relieve 7 R.I.R. in front line trenches.	
11:30	One man hit by shrapnel owing to R.E. officer & sapper unnecessarily exposing themselves on top of the parapet. During the day R.E. sent one N.C.O. and two men down a shaft where our last bore exploded, all three gassed, one badly the others slightly.	
14.00	Batt. Observing Officer reported to B.H.q. Companies were stationed as follows:— Relief of 7th R.I.R. commenced. W. Coy. Enclosure Right Subsector. X. Coy. VILLAGE LINES. Y. Coy. DUKE STREET. Z. Coy. Enclosure Right Subsector.	
18.00	Relief completed. Coys in Village Right Z Coy Centre X Coy Left Y Coy Reserve W Coy. This arrangement was practically reversed on the time in LOOS. left to exception that W x Z changed place. While relief was taking place Stokes Guns fired a few rounds to which the Enemy replied with Rifle grenades and a few heavy T.M. No Damage.	
15.00	Another Officer patrol went out at 12:40 and reconnoitred left of SEAFORTH Crater. It was unoccupied. Men were seen in the GREEN mound into left of GORDON alley. The Bombers boxed them up. At midnight a German working party was surprised by Mills Cup. (D'Arcy)	Batt Sheep H off 43 or 977 Casualties 2 wounded 3 gassed. 49 loss due to Gentlemen and reject of R.E.
15th June LOOS (Left Subsector)	In the Reserve trenches were quiet. a few aerial torpedoes & rifle grenades fired without effect. Two men of the Enemy were observed opposite Down 47 head on by sentries, one man was seen to drop. Enemy snipers attacked wires pretty but more	
02.00	men were seen to drop. and Caroline.	

Army Form C. 2118.

V

WAR DIARY
or
INTELLIGENCE SUMMARY

(Erase heading not required.)

1st Royal Munster Fus.

1916	Hour, Date, Place	Summary of Events and Information	Remarks and references to Appendices
15th June (continued)	02.00 to 03.00	Stokes gun dispersed party of Enemy behind NEW Crater. (Capt Pardo I.C.) (Left Coy.) Enemy opened rapid Rifle fire with Artillery H.E. & shrapnel (moderate fire Minutes. (Capt Pearce) V Coy.	
	06.00 to 18.30	Mills grenades and rifle grenades were fired by us throughout the night. (Capt Bekes Z Coy) Generally quiet during the day. Enemy of the CAMERON rally every quarter of an hour with rifle fire, grenades. Also fired heavy T.M. a short line Bay 53 Elem in. (Capt Pardo I.C.)	
	17.45	About 30 large bombs were fired by the Germans	
	20.10	Enemy fired several torpedoes. For 2½ Cwt, we replied with rifle grenades (approximately 54).	Batt. Strength. Off 43 or 973 Casualties. Nil
	23.00	Enemy fired about 40 torpedoes, which fell up to enemy wire, and repaired two working parties in enemy trench	
16th June LOOS. (left subsector)	12.45	Lewis Gun dispersed a party of the enemy on top behind new Crater and on our Lt. (2-Lt Hussey)	
		Hand grenades were thrown from new Crater. We fell short, we replied with rifle grenades.	
		Germans were seen in between Craters S. of SEAFORTH Crater. Dispersed by rifle grenades and Mills Rnds.	
		Several small parties of the enemy came out of New Crater between SEAFORTH Crater and the New Crater but were driven back by Lewis Guns & bombs	
	01.00	Enemy started throwing hand grenades around working party in front of new Crater, we replied with rifle grenades, and bombs & 4.5 Stokes Guns. No more trouble during the night. (2-Lt Veing. Bombers)	
	02.20	Three heavy bombs were fired & about 6 ordinary bombs (Capt Pardon X Coy)	
	03.30	Enemy artillery fires several shells along ENGLISH Alley up to support line	
		During the night Enemy fired M.G. bursts along our parapet.	
	07.30	Enemy first change T.M. (in about 20 minutes we replied with T.M. Enemy ceased.	

VI

WAR DIARY
or
INTELLIGENCE SUMMARY
(Erase heading not required.)

Army Form C. 2118.

1st Royal Munsters B——

Instructions regarding War Diaries and Intelligence Summaries are contained in F. S. Regs., Part II. and the Staff Manual respectively. Title pages will be prepared in manuscript.

Hour, Date, Place		Summary of Events and Information	Remarks and references to Appendices
1916			
16th June (Cameron)	16.00	Enemy shelled CAMERON Alley intermittently for 1 hr and a half from 17.00. Enemy shelled our front line with heavy T.M. (Cerche Company) and Bay. Flown in. No damage done. Our T.M. retaliates	Batt Strength. Off 43 or 973. Casualties. 1 wounded. 2 wounded and died from the effects a few hours.
	18.00	Enemy sent out about 50 heavy T.M. Trench Grenades & Bombs in at Bay 37	
	21.30	Intermittent M.G. fire and sniping by the enemy till 4 am. Enemy party attempting to work on parapet were driven in by Lewis Guns and grenades.	
	19.30	Gordon alley blown in by enemy at Heavy TOPx also a portion of English Alley blown in. Our working parties privately fired on by Enemy M.G. We retaliated with Lewis Guns on German working with good results. No shoots and forms were heard. Enemy made no further attempt at working or wire. German Trench Guns reported. Scott Alley.	
17th June LOOS. (left subsector)	22.00 02.15	Enemy developed from New Crater by Bombers and Stokes guns. Enemy Threw aerial torpedoes and Rifle grenades, we replied with Stokes guns and rifle grenades.	Batt Strength. Off 43 or 966. Casualties. 6 wounded. 1 Accidentally wounded by explosion of 6 fuse.
	04.30	German Band heard playing opposite Scotts Alley. During the day fairly quiet. Enemy shelled parts of LOOS area.	
	20.30	WELSH Alley to Souvage was done.	
	22.30	Relief by 6th R.Dub. Reg. Commenced. " " " " Completed.	
18th June MAZINGARBE	12.30	Batt marched to MAZINGARBE Hut Camp and arrived about 12.30 am. Nothing to record	Batt Strength Off 43 or 957 Casualties Nil

Army Form C. 2118.

1st R Munster Fusiliers

WAR DIARY
or
INTELLIGENCE SUMMARY
(Erase heading not required.)

Hour, Date, Place		Summary of Events and Information	Remarks and references to Appendices
1916			
19th June. MAZINGARBE.		In Billets. Nothing to report except inspection by Army Commander at NOEUX-LES-MINES.	Batt Strength Off 42 or 957. Casualties Nil.
20th June	09.30	Enemy sent several shells into MAZINGARBE. Some of which fell in the huts where troops were billeted. Four men were wounded.	Batt Strength Off 43 - or 952. Casualties 4 wounded.
	10.00	Capt & Qr Baxter reported for duty from U.K. (6th Battalion RMF)	
21st June		2nd Lt J. Cooke reported for arrival from 2nd Batt (RMF) Nothing to record.	Batt Strength Off 44 or 946. Casualties nil.
22nd June	09.30	Enemy dropped several shells along road by R.C. Camp. 2nd Lt Smith + 2nd Lt Cooke wounded and one man. Nothing further to record	Batt Strength Off 44 or 941. Casualties Off 2 or 1.
		Nothing to record.	Batt Strength Off 44 or 936. Casualties nil.
23rd June			Batt Strength Off 45 or 953. Casualties nil.
24th June		Lieut Beatty reported for duty from 2nd Res RMF.	Batt Strength Off 45 or 931. Casualties nil.
25th June		Nothing to record.	Batt Strength Off or Casualties nil
~~26th~~ June		~~Nothing to report~~	
26th June MAZINGARBE	18.00	Under orders to move out at 18.00 and proceed to Pont 14 Bis Right Sub sector.	Batt Strength Off 45 or 932. Casualties nil.
	20.30	Batt marched out by companies. Relief of 7th R.I. Fus commenced.	
	23.00	Relief completed.	
27th June Pont 14 Bis (Left Sub sector)	00.45	Large mine was exploded in S. of LOOS Crassier. Very heavy Artillery duel on the right extending on the Right Flank as far as the Right Coy of the Battalion. The 8th Dublin & Right Sub-sector Co's were engaged in an attempt to seize the crater. The Artillery continued through the night but on the Right Coy to the Batt ceased at 16.45. A certain amount of damage was done + our trenches were somewhat on the Right, the Left was comparatively quiet.	

VIII

Army Form C. 2118.

WAR DIARY
or
INTELLIGENCE SUMMARY
(Erase heading not required.)

13th P. Munster Fus.

Hour, Date, Place	Summary of Events and Information	Remarks and references to Appendices
27th June Pont 14 Bis (Left subsector) (Continued)	During the day everything quiet. Reconnoitering situations were made (a 15 neighty 27-28) and carried out with the exception that I.M. were not employed with the result that the operations on our particular front were ineffective so far as our infantry were concerned, nor do I think that any material damage was effected by its Artillery.	Batt Strength O/r 45 x O/R 928. Casualties O/R 4 wounded.
23.00	Patrol went out to reconnoitre out and wire and stake Enemy's new front line Batt. Reported when gaps were cut wire and stakes Enemy's wire partly cut down.	
28th June Pont 14 Bis (Left subsector) 01.00 / 01.10	Artillery Bombardment of Enemy's trenches and communication trenches. Smoke clouds were sent up all along our front, at the same time Artillery increased.	
01.20	Rate of fire of fire till 01.20. Smoke continued. Artillery fire continued.	
01.40	Artillery fire lifted and made barrage behind the Enemy's lines, while Lewis Guns kept gaps in Enemy's wire open.	
01.45	Patrol under Lt Beatty went over the parapet, crossed our wire and advanced towards supposed gap in German wire. Party consisting of 2/Lt Beatty, 1 Sergeant, 1 Corporal and 12 men. Advanced about 150x but found this ground to have no German line. was heard & called. Party only lay out till 2.15 waiting for Artillery to cease ground was clear when to part was out.	
02.30	Party recrossed our parapet according to instructions.	
02.45	Artillery fire ceased. Remainder of night quiet. Some bombers were damaged. Enemy's bombers were damaged. strange damage slight.	
21.00	Two patrols went out one to Right Coy and one from the Left Coy as reports on the Enemy wire. 2/Lt Callaghan & 2/Lt Sandom 2 Coy., along Bois front followed by shrapnel. Tried	
26.00	Rifle & Lewis gun fire for two minutes along Bois front followed by shrapnel. Tried trench - Rifle Grenades fire for 5 minutes. No Lewis or rapid rifle fire in the enemy's right trenches and went great rapidity into T.M's & Rifle Grenades and shrapnel. Enemy retaliated	

1247 W 3299 200,000 (E) 8/14 J.B.C.& A. Form C. 2118/13.

Army Form C. 2118.

WAR DIARY
or
INTELLIGENCE SUMMARY

(Erase heading not required.)

1st Royal Munster Fus.

Hour, Date, Place	Summary of Events and Information	Remarks and references to Appendices
1916		
26th June. Pont 14 Bis (Continued)	Trenches on the left, front line and support and communication trenches were badly damaged. Considerable damage was done all along the front but the left was worst.	Batt. Strength. O/f 45 or 924 Casualties Killed (Rapesz) 8 Wounded 3
18.30	During the day everything was fairly quiet. The enemy shelled the Right and Centre Company support line heavily, the communication trench and support line was badly damaged. Bombardment of Cpl Peirce's sap at B Coy. The centre was dealt with about 22:00 and continued to go German wire till 300 pm.	
24th June Pont 14 Bis		
01.30	Recce patrols went out and reconnoitred the German wire and were fired on by 1 and 2 guns. Enemy were seen working on and round their trenches. During the day everything was comparatively quiet.	
	Orders received that Batt would be relieved by 2. R.I. Rifles.	Batt. Strength 45 O/f 920 O.R. Casualties 2 Killed 1 O.R.
18.00	During the day things were comparatively quiet. Enemy again shelled the support line on the Right and Chalk Pit alley at the junction of support line and Chalk pit alley.	Batt Strength 45 O/f 894 O.R. Casualties R.M.O. 2 Wounded 6
18.15	Relief commenced.	
9.10	Relief completed.	
TENTH AVENUE 10.00	Battalion in Brigade Support.	
30th June TENTH AVENUE	Nothing to record.	

R. Maude Mason Lt Col
Commanding 1st R Munster Fus

WAR DIARY

1st Battalion
Royal Munster
Fusiliers

1st. July to 31st. July 1916.

VOLUME No. ?

Page 1

Army Form C. 2118.

WAR DIARY
or
INTELLIGENCE SUMMARY.
(Erase heading not required.)

1st Bn. Royal Munster Fusiliers

Instructions regarding War Diaries and Intelligence Summaries are contained in F. S. Regs., Part II. and the Staff Manual respectively. Title pages will be prepared in manuscript.

Place	Date	Hour	Summary of Events and Information	Remarks and references to Appendices
	JULY JUNE			
10TH AVENUE 14 BIS SECT.	1ST	—	Battalion in Bn. Support line relieved 8 Officers 1200 O.R. Noeux Les Mines	
"	3RD	—	Battalion moved into Right Sub Sect. 14 Bis at 17:00 in relief of 7th R.I. Rifles	Appendix A
			Relief complete 21:30.	Appendix B
RIGHT SUB SECT. 14 BIS SECT.	4TH	—	48th D.S.H. Enterprise	
"	6TH	2040	Enemy open intense bombardment on front support & reserve trenches	
"	7TH		Battn moved into Bn. Reserve in Billets at PHILOSOPHE W. being relieved by 7th R.I. Rifles in the trenches & taking over billets from 7th R.I. Rifles	
PHILOSOPHE	8TH		Battn found carrying parties in trenches 11 offs. 400 O.R.	
"	9TH		" " " " " "	
"	11TH	10:00	Battn was relieved by 8th R.M.F. & marched to Noeux Les Mines to refit	Billets.
NOEUX LES MINES	18TH		Lewis Gun Battn. relieved Lewis Gun Sec. of 7th Munster's Wing in Loos Section	
"	19TH		Battn. relieved 7th Bn. Munster's Wing Division in the Left Sub Section Loos Section	
LEFT SUB SECT. LOOS SECT.	22ND		Battn was relieved by 12th Suffolk Regt. & proceeded to MAZINGARBE	
MAZINGARBE	24TH		Battn relieved 7th Bn. Munster's Fusiliers in Centre Sub Sect. Hulluch Sect.	
CENTRE SUB SECT. HULLUCH	27TH	15:20	Enemy blew a mine opposite front line trench between Bayeaux 81-82 (no casualties). Enemy attempted to rush the crater but were repulsed.	Appendix C
			(See attached report)	

WAR DIARY
INTELLIGENCE SUMMARY

Army Form C. 2118.
Page 2
1st Bn. Munster Fusiliers

Place	Date	Hour	Summary of Events and Information	Remarks and references to Appendices
CENTRE SUB SECT. HULLUCH SECT.	JULY 27th		During the night two sections R.E. were sent up & with their assistance two new saps were dug towards the crater	
"	28th	02.00	Enemy attempted to enter our trench N. of BRECON SAP but were driven off having two large tin boxes connected with electric wires under our wire (These boxes were brought in & forwarded to Army H.Q. the following night). Batt. were relieved by 9th Bn. Dublin Fusiliers & proceeded to support in CRESCENT in Bgde. reserve. Lieut Hodge made a reconnaissance behind the new crater & Lieut Beatty executed a small raid on enemy line H7.a.14. Casualty return for the month.	Appendix D Appendix D Appendix E

R Markham Lt Col
Capt 1 R Munster R
1/8/16

48th Bde. No. S.L.S./G. 50.

SECRET.

Appendix A

Major WILSON, 1st Munsters.   7th Irish Rifles)
8th Dublins.   Staff Captain   )   For
9th Dublins.   48th M.G. Company)   information.
1st Munsters.   48th T.M. Battery)

1. Smoke will be discharged from the Brigade Front in conjunction with L.W's. on the Night of the 4/5th July, during the operation to be carried out that Night.

2. L.W's. *with Smoke* will be discharged at 11.0 P.M. ~~The discharge of Smoke will begin at 1.0 A.M. on the 5th instant and will last about 10 minutes.~~

3. The method and organisation for the discharge of Smoke will be exactly similar to that laid down in Brigade No. S.L.S./G. 19, dated 26.6.16 and S.L.S./G. 43 dated 2.7.16.

   Sections 2 and 3A will be found by the 1st Munsters.
   Sections 3 and 4 will be found by the 9th Dublins.

4. The Staff Captain will arrange for the necessary amount of Stores to be issued to O.C. Units concern[ed]

Captain,
Brigade Major, 48th Infant[ry]

2nd July, 1916.

2.

Equipment of above parties is given in the Appendix.

4. PLAN.

(a) The enemy's front line trenches will be subjected to an intense bombardment of about 10 minutes (details and extent have yet to be arranged). Prior to the bombardment the columns will have previously left our trenches and be lying out about 100 yards in front of our wire in the following formation :-

    1. Torpedo Party.
    2. Covering Party.
    3. Blocking Party.
    4. Assaulting Party.

(b) At half time of the bombardment, Smoke will be let off from our front trenches in rear of the columns and a Smoke barrage put up on each flank by Trench Mortars. At the same time the Covering Parties will set off Smoke Candles.

(c) Under cover of the Smoke, the Torpedo and Covering Party will advance towards the enemy's wire as near as the Artillery fire will permit, the Assaulting Parties following them at an interval.

(d) At a stated time the Artillery Barrage will lift and concentrate on the areas marked "T" and "S" on attached Map and will continue on the enemy's front line on the flanks. At this moment the Torpedo Party will advance and destroy the enemy's wire.

(e) The explosion of the BANGALORE TORPEDO of a Column will be the Signal for that column to assault.

(f) The following will be the action of each Column in the ASSAULT.

  (i) LEFT Column.

    (a) Blocking Party on entering trench at "A" turn to the left and establish a block about 50 yards beyond Sap 7 (Point W. on Map). This Party will raid and bomb any dug-outs encountered en route.

    (b) LEFT ASSAULTING PARTY will cross over the enemy's front line trenches at Point "A", and search dug-outs, emplacements, etc. in PUITS 14 BIS. This party having carried out its mission will retrun to Point "A" and thence back by the same route to trenches.

    (c) RIGHT ASSAULTING PARTY. will turn to the Right after entering trench at Point "A" and work down the trench to Point "B" where it will leave the trenches and return to our trenches passing through the Covering Party of the CENTRE Column and following the tape laid out by them.

    (d) The COVERING Party will remain at Point "A" and will arrange to evacuate to our trenches at once any prisoners, wounded or loot.

3.

(ii) CENTRE Column.

(a) The BLOCKING Party. The Blocking Party will block the Boyau at Point "X".

(b) The COVERING Party will remain at Point "B" and cover the withdrawal of the Right Assaulting Party Left Column.

(iii) RIGHT Column.

(a) Right Blocking will enter trench at "C" and turn to its right and establish a block just South of Sap 3 at Point "Z".

(b) Left Blocking Party will enter trench at "C" turn to its left and then to the Right up the first Boyau and establish a block at Point "Y".

(c) The Assaulting Party will turn to its Left at "A" and clear the front line trench towards "B", and will xxxx withdraw through Point "B".

(d) The Covering Party will remain at Point "C" and cover the withdrawal of the Blocking Parties at "Y" and "Z".

NOTE. All BLOCKING PARTIES will search dug-outs met with and send any Prisoners, Guns captured, etc., immediately to nearest Covering Party.

(g) Arrangements for withdrawal.

The Assaulting Parties on completion of their mission will report to the Covering Party through which they withdraw. As soon as all these Parties are clear, O.C. Covering Parties will let off two Fumite Grenades as a Signal for the Blocking Parties to withdraw. Each Blocking Party will on leaving its position fire one Fumite Bomb in acknowledgment to their signal (The Bombs must be fired on top on the ground and not in the trench) In the event of no acknowledgment being forthcoming the Covering Party will xxx repeat the signal.

As soon as the Blocking Parties are clear the Covering Parties will then withdraw.

(h) The Torpedo Parties, after the destruction of the wire, will withdraw along the tape brought out by the Covering Party and form a line of Connecting files to assist in the direction of withdrawal.

(j) No time will be laid down for the duration of the Enterprise but the time spent in the hostile trenches should not exceed 20 minutes.

Appendix B 6

SITUATION REPORT.

on 6th July 16

At 8-40 p.m. the enemy opened an intense bombardment on our front line, support and reserve trenches. The fire was concentrated chiefly in the following area.

Front line Boyah 54 to Boyah 61, and the support line immediately in rear. Meath Trench and reserve line from Hugo Lane to the North, but exactly how far I have not been able to ascertain.

Whether the fire extended in to the left subsection to any extent I do not know. At 9-15 the bombardment lifted but a certain amount was still in the area stated above.

At 9-25 the bombardment slackened.

At 1000 the bombardment was only intermittent.

At 10-5 the situation was quiet.

At 10-40 there was a short burst of shrapnel on the support line and reserve line. Since which time the situation has been quiet.

Our artillery retaliated at 8-47 p.m. and continued until the Leason Officer reported situation normal at 10-5 p.m.

At the same time as the burst of shrapnel trench mortars were fired by the enemy.

At 10-30 p.m. I proceeded to inspect the lines. The front line from Boyan 54 to Boyan 61 is seriously damaged and practically non-existent as a fire trench.

Boyan 52 is absolutely blocked.

Boyan 54 badly damaged and quite exposed on the N for about 20 yards, and the Boyans N of this in much the same condition. The communication between Boyan 57 and 59 in rear of the blind bit of trench is entirely cut off.

Every available man is clearing the trenches, but I do not think that the connection between Boyan 56 and 59 can be completed to-night.

There was no raid by the enemy.*

12-55 a.m
7/7/16.

(signed) R. Monck-Mason Lt-Col.
Comdg. 1st. Royal Munster Fusiliers.

* It has since been ascertained that the enemy entered the battered trenches between Boyaus 56 - 59 but were forced to leave immediately without inflicting any damage.

T.E. Nelson Maj
1st RMF

Appendix B 7

REPORT ON ATTEMPTED ENEMY RAID.
on 6th July

At about 9-15 p.m, when the enemy's fire lifted, 2/Lieut J.S. Jowett was on duty in the front line trench of the left Company. He was at the right of Boyan 56, he gave orders for 13 and 14 Platoons who had taken cover in listening galleries to stand to, and was proceeding to No.16 Platoon which was on the left of Boyan 56, when he met two men of the Dublin Fusiliers who had been working at the mine shafts, rushing along the trench, they told 2/Lt. Jowett that the Germans were in the trench.

2/Lt. Jowett formed a bombing party at once from the men he had with him and ran along the trench, on his way he met Sgt. Bridgman who made the same statement as the men of the Dublins.

The party proceeded along the trench and could find no trace of the enemy.

This morning Major Wilson on going round found three German bombs, one unexploded and one in a small dug out.

I have not been able to find anyone who actually saw any Germans, but the fact of the small dug out mentioned having been bombed shows that the enemy must have entered.

The dug out is on the parapet side of the trench and in between Boyans 56 and 57.

What evidently happened is that a very small party, probably not more than two or three of the enemy must have crawled up jumped into the trench thrown a few bombs and returned.

There was only one man Pte. Tuohy in the dug out bombed.

There is no evidence that the enemy succeeded in taking anything away with them.

The only proof of the enemy having entered is the finding of the Bombs.

The bombs found are the ordinary hand grenades with wooden handles.

(signed) R. Monck-Mason Lt-Col,

7/7/16.   Comdg. 1st. R. Munster Fusiliers.

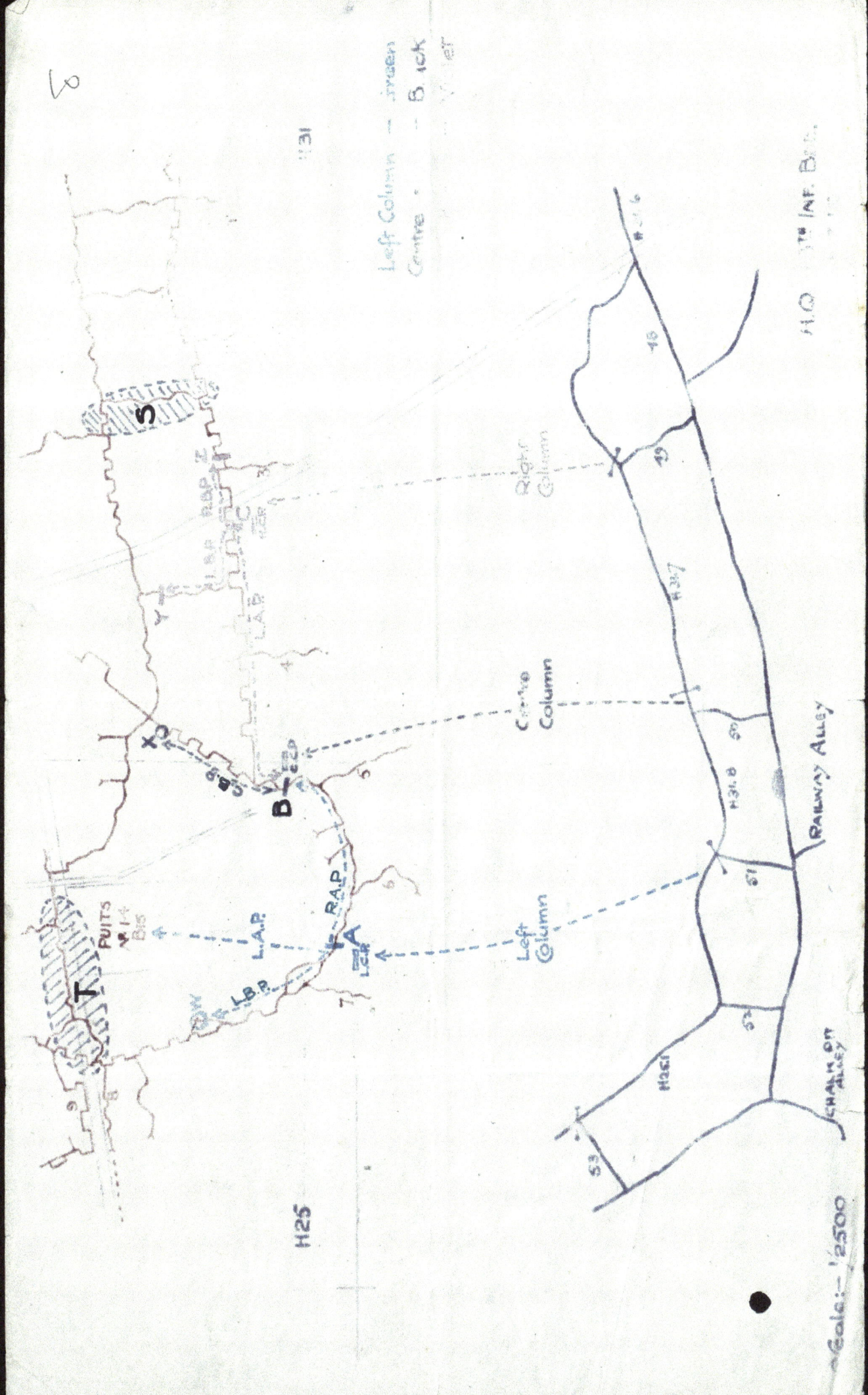

Belgrad

Report on New Crater   Appendix C 9

At about 3.30 pm 27.7.16 the Enemy exploded a mine at a point between Bayonets 81 & 82 NE of BRECON Sap and SE of ASSAYE Crater. The Enemy immediately sent a party of 8 or 10 men armed with bombs to occupy the new crater.

The mine explosion was a complete surprise.

Capt Stewart and Pte Donoghue who were on duty at the end of the sap immediately attacked the enemy with bombs and drove them off. The Enemy dropped their bombs and fled.

We immediately made the necessary arrangements and control the near lip of the crater which is about 15ft from our front line.

About 30ft of our trench was blown in a digging party was at once organized by OC Z Coy.

I propose to consolidate our position tonight. Two saps will be dug to the new crater and Gipsy Land Sap will have to be cleared. Brecon Sap is also much damaged.

I have issued orders for plans for the new saps to be prepared as soon as possible.

Appendix C1

In connection with the above I cannot speak too highly of the conduct of Corp¹ Stewart.

As soon as the mines went up he summed up the situation at a glance and it was due to his initiative that the Enemy attack was repulsed, enabling us to control the near lip of the crater. He was ably supported by Pte Donoghue who also deserves great credit.

The sap these men were in was badly damaged and the occupants much shaken and covered with showers of earth.

R Monck-Mason Lt Col
Comdg 1st R Munster F

27-7-16

Appendix D

71

Report on Operations of the
night of 27-28 July 1916

I propose to give these under three separate
headings.

1/ I issued orders for 2 Lieut Hodges to
execute a raid behind the new craters
and to report on what work the Enemy
were doing.

2nd Lt Hodges and Cpl Stewart went out
at 11.30 and reconnoitred round the S of
the new craters and halfway round the
ASSAYE craters. While there he heard
Lewis Gun bullets striking quite close to
him, so he returned to ascertain the
cause. On his way back he heard cries
and a voice calling out HAMBURG
several times. On returning to the trench
he met the Lewis Gun Officer who told
him he had seen a party of Germans
working in the wire and had opened
fire, and that the Germans had fled.
A party was sent The Enemy opened
a heavy bombardment with T.Ms and
rifle grenades on our trenches and round
the craters so that it was not possible
for the 2nd Lt Hodges party to go out, so
the raid was abandoned. The fire
extended from B.9 craters to D.1.53.

2 Lieut Hodges saw and heard no enemy working parties.

Appendix D? 12

2. At about 12 midnight Lieut McVeigh was with one of his Lewis Guns just on the Right of BRECON Sap. The Corporal drew his attention to the fact that there was something moving in our wire. He sent up a Very light and could see two hands working on the wire just to the Right of BRECON Sap.
He ordered the Corporal to open fire, and about 12 men jumped up and started running towards the German lines. We fired on them, and 2/Lieut Baily threw hand grenades into the wire.
The Corporal states that he saw two men fall. One of the Enemy shouted HAMBURG several times in a loud voice.
A few minutes later Lt McVeigh states that he saw two men trying to crawl away, they were fired on and no sign of them was afterwards seen.
The Enemy then commenced [a heavy] bombard] ment with TMs and Rifle grenades.
A little later at about 2.30 a.m. when things had quieted down a little I went out with a Corporal and another man to see if any bodies or identifications could be found. He went part of the way through our wire but could

Appendix D 2

get right through at that point. There were about 30 German hand grenades under the wire, and two black oblong bars about the shape of a petrol tin but bigger, with cords attached to them. He tried to lift one but it was too heavy. ~~And was getting day light & then return~~ As it was then getting light Pte McVeigh returned to our trenches.

R Meurik Macm? L/Col
Comm.y 1 R N Z

P.S. On the following night Pte McVeigh again went out and searched the vicinity following tracks as far as the German wire, but could find no bodies. He brought back two tins which were exactly as he described them. I forwarded them to Bde HQ. 4th D?n

3. A small raid was carried out by ~~2 Lieut~~ Beatty on the German trenches at ~~Hay 14~~ H.7. a 1.4.

Lieut Beatty with 10 men armed with bombs and Knobkerries went over the parapet at 1.30 and arrived at the Enemy's wire where a gap had been reported. He found that the wire was thick

Appendix D 3   14

but low and hidden in the long grass, and was unable to get through it. He heard voices in the trench which was about 20' away, and his party immediately threw bombs into the trench. The enemy retaliated and the encounter continued until 2Lt Beatty's supply of bombs were exhausted. The men returned. He reports that he found 3 snipers posts made in shell holes. They were sloped back, and there was a white tape laid from the posts to the German wire. Whether it went through the wire he could not see owing to the long grass, but there was no gap in the wire where the tapes ended. and it was too low to crawl under, and too thick to walk over with any ease.

Lieut Beatty was slightly wounded in both hands and the front of the thigh from bomb splinters. One man was also slightly wounded.

The party were able to throw most of their bombs into the trench.

R Monkhouse Lieut Col
Comdg 1st R Munster Fus

25-7-16.

Appendix E

DAILY STRENGTH AND CASUALTIES FOR JULY 1916

	O	O.R.	
1st.	45	881	4 O.R. Joined, 8 O.R. to Hosp. 5 O.R. Wd.
2nd.	45	872	8 O.R. to Hosp.
3rd.	45	864	4 O.R. Wd. 2 O.R. to Hosp.
4th.	45	858	2 O.R. Wd., 2 O.R. to Hosp.
5th.	45	854	5 O.R. Wd. 4 O.R. to Hosp.
6th.	45	845	Lieut. Hicks Wd. 9 O.R. Wd. 1 O.R. Killed. 1 O.R. to Hosp.
7th.	44	834	3 Offrs. killed (Capt. Murray, 2nd. Lt. King, 2nd. Lt. Harold-Barry,) 2nd. Lt. O'Callaghan Wd. 2 O.R. Killed 2 O.R. Missing. 17 O.R. Wd.
8th.	40	813	Lt. Smith and 2nd. Lt. Cooke to U.K. (Struck off). Draft of 10 O.R. 1 O.R. Wd. 1 O.R. Hosp.
9th.	38	821	1 O.R. to Hosp. 1 O.R. Wounded.
10th.	38	819	
11th.	38	819	1 O.R. Wounded.
12th.	38	818	1 O.R. Transferred to R.E's. 3 O.R. Hosp.
13th.	38	814	4 O.R. Hosp.
14th.	38	810	1 O.R. to Hosp.
15th.	38	809	10 O.R. rejoined. 3 O.R. Draft. 4 O.R. Hosp.
16th.	38	818	
17th.	38	818	3 O.R. Hosp.
18th.	38	815	3 O.R. Wd. 6 O.R. Hosp.
19th.	38	806	6 O.R. Wounded.
20th.	38	800	2nd. Lt. C.J. Murphy Killed, Lt. F.E. Furney Wd. 8 O.R. Wd. 7 O.R. Hosp.
21st.	36	785	1 O.R. Killed. 1 O.R. Hosp. 5 Offrs. reported for duty from 3rd. R.M.Fus.
22nd.	41	783	2 O.R. Killed. 3 O.R. Wd., 1 O.R. Hosp.
23rd.	41	777	2nd. Lt. Hansell to U.K. (Struck Off).
24th.	40	777	2nd. Lt. Haymen to U.K. (Struck Off). 3 Offrs. reported for duty from 3rd. R.M.Fus.
25th.	42	777	2nd. Lt. Hartnett (Struck Off) 2 O.R. Wd.
26th.	41	775	1 O.R. Killed. 2 O.R. Wd. 1 O.R. Hosp.
27th.	41	771	2nd. Lt. Prendergast Killed, 1 O.R. Wd. 8 O.R. Hosp.
28th.	40	762	2 O.R. Killed. 4 O.R. Wd. 2 O.R. Hosp.

	O	O.R.	
29th.	40	754	
30th.	40	754	2 O.R. Hospital.
			1 Offr. reported for duty from 6th. Conn. Rgrs.
31st.	41	752	

Vol 6

48/6

WAR DIARY.

1st Royal Munster Fusiliers

MONTH OF AUGUST, 1916.

VOLUME:-

Army Form C. 2118.

WAR DIARY
or
INTELLIGENCE SUMMARY.
(Erase heading not required.)

1st Batt. R.M. Munster Fusiliers
Aupier - 1916

Instructions regarding War Diaries and Intelligence Summaries are contained in F.S. Regs., Part II. and the Staff Manual respectively. Title pages will be prepared in manuscript.

Place	Date	Hour	Summary of Events and Information	Remarks and references to Appendices
	AUGUST			
RIGHT SUB SECT HULLUCH	1st		Batt. relieved 7th Batt. Rl. Irish Rifles - Relief complete 3 p.m.	Appendix
"	4th		48th Bgde raid on enemy trenches	Appendix B
"	8th		Batt. moves to Bgde. Reserve at PHILOSOPHE WEST	Appendix C
PHILOSOPHE W.	12th		Batt. relieved 2nd Batt. Rl. Irish Rifles - LEFT SUB SECT HULLUCH	Appendix
LEFT SUB SECT HULLUCH	18th		Batt. relieved by 7th Batt. Rl. Irish Rifles & proceeded to TENTH AVENUE in relief of 8th Rl. Dublin Fus.	Appendix
TENTH AVENUE	20th		Batt. relieved 7th Rl. Irish Rifles in LEFT SUB SECT HULLUCH	Appendix
			Batt. raid on enemy trenches in conjunction with other Bgts. of the Bgde.	Appendix G
LEFT SUB SECT HULLUCH	24th		Batt. was relieved by 17th Batt. H.L.I. (9th Rgt. Div.) & proceeded to relief at PHILOSOPHE	Appendix
PHILOSOPHE	25th	08.00	Batt. left PHILOSOPHE & proceeded by march route via MAZINGARBE - NUEUX LES MINES - BRUAY - MARLES LES MINES - LOZINGHEM to ALLOUAGNE arr 5 p.m.	Appendix J
ALLOUAGNE	29th	19.30	Batt. left & marched to village CHOCQUES arr. 21.00. Entrained (Staff in command)	Appendix
LONGUEAU MINICAMP	30th	06.30	Train arr. Y Batt. detrained & marched by VILLERS-BRETONNEUX - FOUILLOY	
		13.45	to CORBIE	
CORBIE	31st	11.45	Batt. left & with 48th Inf. Bgde marched via MERICOURT L'ABBE - VILLE-SOUS-CORBIE to the "SANDPIT" G XIVth Corps Reserve Division area arr. 19.00	Appendix

Appendix B

To:-
    Headquarters,
        48th. Infantry Brigade.

I beg to submit the following report on Operations on the night of the 4th. and 5th. August 1916.

As soon as it was dark enough at about 10.45 or 11 p.m. four out of the six torpedoes proceeded to be taken out.

The other two belonging to parties No. 5 & 6 were unable to go out as somehow they miscarried; full inquiry will be made; they were sent down at the same time as the others from Battn, Headquarters.

At 11.54 p.m. No. 1 Torpedo was reported in position and at 12.23 No. 2 was reported in position. At 12.23 the order came from the Brigade "Retard 30 minutes" I sent runners off at once but they were too late to stop their torpedoes from being exploded. No. 1 was exploded exactly at 12.30 and No. 2 at 12.33.

At 12.38 I received a further order "Retard further 15 minutes and at 12.56 another message saying "Retard further 30 minutes!" At 1.33 the message "Carry on" was received which was sent on immediately to the parties concerned.

At 1.45 the Artillery Bombardment started.

Parties 1, 2, 3, 4 and 6 who were lying out in "No Man's Land" immediately went forward. No. 1 party found about 15 to 20 feet of the wire cut and beyond that was thick low wire. The mats were not long enough to span it and owing to the heavy bombing of the enemy only a very small portion was able to be cut. The party engaged the enemy and a bombing engage--ment ensued for about 20 minutes until the bombs were exhausted, when the party returned.

No. 2 party found the gap about 15 feet wide, and almost through the wire, the remainder was crossed by means of mats. The party entered the Sap and searched it thoroughly but could

1

find nothing. They also tried to enter the enemy's front trench but found the neck of the sap entirely blown in and with it a tangled mass of wire from the overhead wire, as the neck end of the Sap had been covered. They were unable to cut their way through, having been there considerably over the time limit. There were no enemy in the vicinity and they were not fired at or bombed.

No. 3 and 4 parties came under a heavy M.G. Fire and Trench Mortars, before they reached the German Wire, and were unable to get forward. They waited out taking cover in shell holes for about half an hour and then returned.

No. 5 party found the wire very thick but only about 18 yards broad. They bombed the Sap from about the centre outwards, there was a machine gun firing from the Sap head and Very Lights were being sent up from the same place.

The Machine Gun was silenced and the Very Lights were not sent up again, neither did any of them show any signs afterwards The party returned after the bombs had been exhausted. The O.C. party found it impossible to cut through the wire in time. The party were apparently secure from the machine gun in the Sap as he did not or could not fire on them. They came under fire of Machine Guns apparently from the N.E.

No. 6 party remained out waiting for the Barage and only came in just before it started. He immediately went to find the Company Commander to ask for instructions, and took some little time finding him and when he returned he saw No. 5 party coming back. This party was on the extreme left and could not very well have got the "Carry On " message in time.

The points attacked were as follows:-

```
No. 1 party      H. 19 a 6 - 7
 "  2 party      H. 13 c 5 - ½
 "  3 party      H. 13 c 5 - ⅔
 "  4 party      H. 13.c 5 - 8
 "  5 party      H. 13 a 3½-2½
```

The German working party that were working between H.13 c 5 - 3 and H. 13 c 5 - 8 did not stop working when No. 1 & 2 Bangalore Torpedoes exploded, as they apparently took the explosion for Shells or T.M's. All Parties reported in by 3.10 a.m.

I attach Copies of Operation. Orders.

(Sgd.) R. H. Monck-Mason, Lt. Colonel,
Comdg. 1st. Battalion Royal Munster Fusiliers.

7.8.16

SECRET.　　　　　　　　　　　　　　　　　　　　　　　　Copy No. 1

Operation Order 24. Appendix C

By Lieut-Col. R.H. Monck-Mason, Comdg. 1st Royal Munster Fusiliers

1. The Battn. will be relieved tomorrow 8th inst. and on relief will be billeted in PHILOSOPHE WEST and will be in Brigade Reserve.
2. Relief will be carried out in accordance with attached table.
3. A Billeting party consisting of Lieut. Kearney, and 1 N.C.O and 1 man per company will proceed to Philosophe to take over billets. They will report to the Adjutant at H.Q at 9-30 a.m for further instructions.
4. Advance parties will arrive to take over trench stores etc at 2 p.m.
5. All kit etc will be dumped at Posern Station by 10 p.m.
6. Receipts for trench stores handed over will be forwarded to Battn. H.Q by 11 a.m 9th inst.
7. Completion of relief of each party to be reported to Battn. H.Q. by code. O.C. Coys. will also report when their Coys. are in billets.
8. Coys. etc. on being relieved will march off independently to billets.
9. W & X Coys will both hand over their trench stores to A Coy. 7th Irish Rifles.

Coy. etc.	Relieving Coy.	Time of relief	Route after relief
1 Platoon Z (Boyau 67-70)	8th Dublins 1 Platoon	10-30 a.m	Essex Lane, 10th Avenue, La Rutoire
3 Platoons Z	C. Coy 7th Irish Rifles	6 p.m.	Hay Alley, 10th Avenue, La Rutoire
W	A Coy. 7th Irish Rifles	5 p.m	do
X	A Coy. 7th Irish Rifles	5 p.m	do
Y	B Coy. 7th Irish Rifles	6 p.m	do
H.Q	H.Q 9th Dublins	11 a.m	La Rutoire (after 2 p.m)
Bombers	7th Irish Rifles	2 p.m	Hay Alley, La Rutoire
Lewis Guns	7th Irish Rifles	5 p.m	do

7-11-16
Issued at:- 6.20 p.m

Appendix G

REPORT ON OPERATIONS ON THE NIGHT OF THE 20th. 21st.
Aug. 1916

I beg to report that the gas and smoke were discharged at the scheduled time. At 11.35 2nd. Lt. Carson went out with the torpedo party and took about five minutes getting to the German wire. The torpedo was placed in position and fired but there was some delay as they could only get two and a half lengths into the wire, the point jammed against something and the torpedo party were unable to force it further, so it was discharged as it was. 2nd. Lt. Callender rushed forward leading the raiding party and found about to 12 to 14 feet of wire uncut. 2nd. Lt. Callender and 2 wire cutters started cutting the wire.

2nd. Lt. Carson reports that when 2nd. Lt. Callender rushed forward he was some way ahead of the men, some of whom missed the gap apparently, and the remainder crowded at the narrow entrance.

The enemy in the meantime had collected and retaliated heavily with bombs, rifle grenades and machine gun fire, snipers were also firing on the party. Men who were outside the wire replied with bombs, and groans were heard coming from the German Trenches. The party remained out for about half an hour, but owing to the heavy fire from the German trenches were unable to get through, and eventually retired.

The party was considerably reduced by casualties.

I think that 2nd. Lt. Callender's conduct deserves great praise, and I believe that had he not outstripped the remainder that in all probability they would have got through. It took 2nd. Lt. Callender about 15 minutes to cut through the wire with the help of one of the wire cutters.

Corporal Murphy was sent back by 2nd. Lt. Callender to get the men together while he was half through the wire, but unfortunately he was wounded. 2nd. Lt. Callender was hit in the back with a dud bomb and slightly wounded in the arm by another.

I believe that the party would have got through had it not been for the delay in having to cut the wire which enabled the enemy to organize their defence.

Casualties.
    3 Officers wounded
    11 men wounded and one man of the Dublins
    4 men missing

I have given orders for a party to be organised to search for the missing men, and the machine gun officer has orders to keep the enemy from repairing their lines.

Major Wilson and Captain Purdon were both slightly gassed but I hope it is not serious. The enemy retaliation when the gas was released was slight, but considerable damage was done to the front trench and Boyau 71

Between 11.5 and 11.45 the enemy did not fire at all.

At 11.25 they again opened fire with Artillery and at 11.40 they sent up red lights and again opened fire. 2nd. Lt. Callender reports that he heard treble voices in the German Trench, evidently boys whose voices had not cracked.

The large number of casualties also helps to account for the party not getting through.

The casualties will be verified to-morrow.

The M.O. informs me that he has attended to ten men, and he has now gone down to the front line to attend to a man who is too bad to be moved.

Our Artillery was very prompt in opening fire.

2nd. Lt. Callender reports that the bomb throwing of the enemy was very wild, they were cleared immediately in front of the gap and attempted to throw from the flanks. The enemy's Machine Guns were the most serious opposition together with the Rifle Grenades.

This raid tends to prove that the enemy Artillery is very weak.

I regret I am not able to report that the raid was successful, but it was not any fault of 2nd. Lts. Callender and Carson, who both behaved admirably, especially the former who showed marked ability and courage.

(sd) R. H. Monck-Mason Lt. Colonel,
Comdg. 1st. Bn. Royal Munster Fusiliers.

21.8.16

SECRET.   OPERATION ORDER No.28.   Copy No:- 1.

Ref. sheet 36 B 1/40000

By Lieut-Col. R.H. Monck-Mason, Comdg. 1st. Royal Munster Fusiliers.

(1) The 48th Brigade will move to-morrow.

(2) The Battn. will move to ALLOUAGNE, by MAZINGARBE, RED ROAD, NOEUX LES MINES, BRUAY, MARLES LES MINES, LOZINGHEM.
Head of column to pass cross roads PHILOSOPHE at 8 a.m.

(3) Order of March.

Companies will parade opposite their billets and march off at the following times:-

    W Coy.   7-45 a.m
    X "   7-55 a.m
    Y "   8-5 a.m
    Z "   8-15 a.m
    Lewis Guns   8-25 a.m.

As far as NOEUX LES MINES a distance of 200 yards will be maintained between platoons.
H.Q. Coy. will march as follows:-
    Signallers and Pioneers at head of W. Coy.
    Snipers with X "
    Bombers with Z "
    Police in rear of Battalion.
1st. Line Transport and baggage wagons will join Battn. at NOEUX.
Cookers will march in rear of their companies until 1st. Line Transport joins the Battn.
There will be a two hours halt for dinners about 12 noon.
O.C. Z. Coy. will detail one officer to march in rear of Battn. and bring on any stragglers.

(4) All packs will be carried on a Motor Lorry and must be stacked ready for loading outside the H.Q. of W. Coy by 6-15 a.m. One storeman per company will load packs at 6-30 a.m. and accompany them on lorry.

(5) A billeting party consisting of 2/Lt. Simpson and one N.C.O or man per company (who can ride a bicycle) will report at H.Q. at 9 p.m. to-night for instructions.

(6) Breakfast will be at 6-30 a.m.

(7) Dress battle order. Caps may be worn after passing NOEUX.

(8) The leading company will halt at cross roads K.16.c 93, for the Battalion to close up.

24 Aug. 1916

Issued at:-

2/Lieut.
a/Adjutant.

CASUALTIES FOR AUGUST 1916.
:-:-:-:-:-:-:-:-:-:-:-:-:-:-:

Aug. 1st.
Strength 41 Offs. 775 O.R.   From Hosp. 3 O.R. To Hosp. 5 O.R.
Aug. 2nd.
Strength 41 Offs. 773 O.R.   From Hosp. 3. Wounded 3. To Hosp. 3.
Aug. 3rd.
Strength 41 Offs. 770 O.R. Wounded 1. To Hospital 3
Aug. 4th.
Strength 41 Offs. 768 O.R. Wounded 2. To Hospital 2.
Aug. 5th.
Strength 41 Offs. 764 O.R. 1 Officer struck off. To Hospital 2 O.R.
                                                        1 O.R. Missing.
Aug. 6th.
Strength 40 Offs. 762 O.R. From Hosp. 2 O.R. Wounded 3 O.R. To Hosp. 2 OR
Aug. 7th.
Strength 40 Offs. 759 O.R.   To Hosp. 2 O.R.
Aug. 8th.
Strength 40 Offs. 757 O.R. Wounded 1 O.R. To Hosp. 1 O.R.
Aug. 9th.
Strength 40 Offs. 755 O.R. Rejoined 2 O.R. To Hosp. 2 O.R.
Aug. 10th.
Strength 40 Offs. 755 O.R. To Hosp. 3 O.R.
Aug. 11th.
Strength 40 Offs. 752 O.R.   To Hosp. 10
Aug. 12th.
Strength 40 Offs. 742 O.R. Transferred 2 O.R. To Hosp. 11 O.R.
Aug. 13th.
Strength 40 Offs. 729 O.R. 1 O.R. Wounded To. Hosp. 3 O.R.
Aug. 14th.
Strength 40 Offs. 725 O.R.   Rejoined 1 O.R.
Aug. 15th.
Strength 40 Offs. 726 O.R. Wounded 8 O.R. To Hosp. 3 O.R.
Aug. 16th.
Strength 40 Offs. 715 O.R. 1 Officer struck off. Wounded 2 O.R. Hosp 5 OR
Aug. 17th.
Strength 39 Offs. 708 O.R.   To Hosp. 1 O.R.
Aug. 18th.
Strength 39 Offs. 707 O.R.
Aug. 19th.
Strength 39 Offs. 707 O.R. Wounded 3 O.R. To Hosp. 4 O.R.
Aug. 20th.
Strength 39 Offs. 700 O.R.
Aug. 21st.
Strength 39 Offs. 700 O.R. Wounded 3 Offs. 27 O.R. Killed 2 O.R. Hosp 2 OR
Aug. 22nd.
Strength 36 Offs. 669 O.R. Rejoined 8 O.R. Wounded 1 Off. 6 O.R. Hosp 6 OR
Aug. 23rd.
Strength 35 Offs. 665 O.R. Rejoined 2 O.R. Wounded 8 O.R. Killed 2 O.R.
                                                         To Hosp. 9 O.R.
Aug. 24th.
Strength 35 Offs. 648 O.R. Wounded 1 O.R. To Hosp. 1 O.R.
Aug. 25th.
Strength 35 Offs. 646 O.R. 2 Offs. Rejoined. Reinforcements 123 O.R.
                                                         To Hosp. 1 O.R.

                        Aug. 26th.
Strength 37 Offs. 768 O.R.   Rejoined 2 O.R.   To Hosp. 3 O.R.

                        Aug. 27th.
Strength 37 Offs. 767 O.R.   To Hosp. 4 O.R.

                        Aug 28th.
Strength 37 Offs. 763 O.R.   To Hosp. 2 O.R.

                        Aug. 29th.
Strength 37 Offs. 761 O.R.   To Hosp. 2 O.R.

                        Aug. 30th.
Strength 37 Offs. 759 O.R.

                        Aug. 31st.
Strength 37 Offs. 759 O.R.

WAR DIARY

1st Royal Munster Fusiliers

FOR MONTH OF SEPTEMBER, 1916.

VOLUME

WAR DIARY or INTELLIGENCE SUMMARY

Army Form C. 2118.

1st Royal Munster Fusiliers September 1916

Place	Date	Hour	Summary of Events and Information	Remarks and references to Appendices
SAND PIT	1st		Batt in Bivouac.	The Battalion Strength does not include all officers not actually serving with the Battalion including Transport officers and not wounded attached
"	2nd		Orders received to move to F.29. S.W. of BILLON FARM on 3rd Sept. and be in Corps Reserve. See Batt. Op Ords No 31. Appendix A. Batt Strength 25 off 649 ot	
			Batt Strength 25 off 649 or	
SW of BILLON FARM.	3rd	9.30	Batt. marched from SAND PIT, to F.29. S.W. of BILLON FARM.	Appendix A
		11.30	Batt arrived at Bivouac F.29. S.W. of BILLON FARM.	
		14.00	Orders received to move to CARNOY.	
		16.30	Batt marched out of F.29 SW of BILLON FARM.	
		15.00	Batt arrived at Bivouac S side of CARNOY Batt Strength 25 off 647 ot	
BERNAFAY BONAFAY WOOD	4th	4.00	Batt received orders to proceed to BERNAFAY WOOD	
		5.00	Batt marched out of CARNOY	
		7.30	Batt arrived BERNAFAY WOOD.	
			The wood and shelters were heavily shelled at intervals during the day, at about 28.00 hr. Enemy bombarded heavily causing many casualties. The Batt HQ shelter was hit by a gas shell and the following officers were gassed and evacuated during the night. Capt C R Williams Capt B H Stephenson, Lieut. J T Murphy, 2 Lieut E F Hussey, 2 Lieut E C Cowley, 2 Lieut CO Catherwood 2 Lieut A G Bisset M.O. 2 Lieut J W Baldwin was evacuated to shell shock + 2 Lt P J Martin (dysentery)	

Army Form C. 2118.

WAR DIARY
or
INTELLIGENCE SUMMARY.
(Erase heading not required.)

"8" R'Grimsley Inn   September 1916

Place	Date	Hour	Summary of Events and Information	Remarks and references to Appendices
TRENCHES facing GINCHY.	8th		Lieut Col R Monck-Mason slightly gassed & evacuated. B.S.M Shergill 25 & 64.7 ev.	
		15:00	At BERNAFAY WOOD. The following officers reported for duty from 3rd R.M.F. Lieut D.S. Maunsell. Lieut R.H. Hudson, 2nd Lieut W.A.G. Nolan, 2nd Lieut J.B. O'Farrell, 2nd Lieut J.H. Ley.	
		16:00	Lieut C. Allinson R.A.M.C. reports for duty vice Lieut A.G. Bissett R.A.M.C. evacuated.	
		17:30	Batt. marched off from BERNAFAY WOOD to relieve the 8th K.R.R.C. in the trenches. The line taken up was astride the railway running E x W south of GINCHY. as follows. From about T.20.c.4.6 to T.20.a.1.4. and hence to T.20.a T.19.b.7.3½. The 9th R.Dublin Fusiliers were in the right with whom we were in touch. We were unable to gain touch with the Batt.n on our left. Our support line ran along the GINCHY - WEDGE WOOD road from the Railway Southward to about T.20.c.2.5. There were two strong points in advance of the line, reconnoitred by army trench at about T.20.a.3.3½ and one about T.19.b.8.5½. The companies were disposed as follows. From Right & Left. W.X.Y.Z all in the front line. W x X Coy. finding the strong points. During the day the trench was heavily shelled by the enemy at intervals but the casualties was slight as the cover was too high. The enemy snipers were active, the following officers being killed during the night Lieut W.F. McCarthy O'Leary, Lieut D.S. Maunsell and	

WAR DIARY
or
INTELLIGENCE SUMMARY.
(Erase heading not required.)

Army Form C. 2118.

1st R. Munster Fus.   September 1916

Place	Date	Hour	Summary of Events and Information	Remarks and references to Appendices
In the Trenches S of GINCHY.	6th	23.00	Lieut R.H. Hudson was slightly shell shocked. Relief completed. Batt. Strength 16 Offrs. 625 o.r. During the day the enemy intermittently shelled the trenches, especially from 11:30 to 2 pm when the shelling was severe, but the casualties few as the aim was too high. The night was fairly quiet. There was great shortage of water but this was brought up soon after dusk. During the night a new trench was dug further forward on the right from the railway cut T.20.a.1.2 to T.20.c.7.7. Straightening out line with the Batt. on our Right. Our left was also extended and a line commenced from T.19.c.7.3½ extending West to the GUILLEMONT-GINCHY Road. Touch was gained with the Batt. on our Left, and shown found that they had dug in too far back about 300 x in rear of our Left flank. Batt. Strength 21 Offs 600 o.r.	
In the Trenches S of GINCHY.	7th		Enemy showed less activity during the day and the shelling was less severe. Orders were received from Bde HQ for the Batt HQ. to move back to the QUARRIES on GUILLEMONT that night, and for the Battalion to move to the Left and prepare and occupy a line from the Railway at T.20.a.1.3 to the GINCHY-GUILLEMONT Road, at T.19.b.3.6. A second line to be dug behind the line, for the supporting Battalion to occupy for the attack. The front line was completed during the night, and the support	

WAR DIARY or INTELLIGENCE SUMMARY

Army Form C. 2118.

IV

1st Royal Munster Fr September 1916

Place	Date	Hour	Summary of Events and Information	Remarks and references to Appendices
BATT HQ CHALK PIT GUILLEMONT Battalion in the Trenches	8th		line was commenced. Batt Strength 15 off. 577 or	
		0.30	Batt. H.Q. moved to CHALK PIT GUILLEMONT 2/RM Batt reported for duty.	
		2.30	Battalion moved to allotted position	
			During the day the Battn. suffered heavy casualties from our own shells which were dropping short. The matter was adjusted but not until several reports had been sent in.	
			During the night the two lines of trenches were completed, the 8th R. Dublin Fusiliers moving into the rear line. The 7/R Irish Rifles moved up on our Right and brought their Left Flank up in line with our right. The Enemy's artillery were not very active. Batt Strength 15 off — 535 or.	
GINCHY	9th		On the morning of the 9th Batt H.Q. moved up to a dug out N of GUILLEMONT at about T.19.c.4.9. Below attack Batt. Strength 13 off. 515 o.r	
		16.45	Attack commenced. Report on operations by O.C. 1R.M.F	
			Appendix B.	Appendix B
			Appendix C. 48th Inf. Brigade Operation order. no 64	" C
			Appendix D. 1st R Munsters Fus. Operation order.	" D
			After attack Batt Strength 5 off 305 o.r	
HAPPY VALLEY	10th		On the morning the Battn. moved into the HAPPY VALLEY. Batt Strength 5 off. 305 or	
CORBY.	11th	12.30	Batt. marched from HAPPY VALLEY	

Army Form C. 2118.

WAR DIARY
or
INTELLIGENCE SUMMARY.
(Erase heading not required.)

1st R Munster Fus — September 1916

Instructions regarding War Diaries and Intelligence Summaries are contained in F.S. Regs., Part II. and the Staff Manual respectively. Title pages will be prepared in manuscript.

Place	Date	Hour	Summary of Events and Information	Remarks and references to Appendices
		15.30	Arrived at CORBIE and went into billets. Also Brig. RAMC reported for duty. Batt Strength 5 off 305 or	Appendix E
CORBIE	12th		Appendix E. Bn Operation Order No 32. Batt Strength 5 off 305 or	
"	13"		In billets. Batt Strength 5 off 301 or	
"	14"		In billets. Batt Strength 5 off 301 or	
"	15"		In billets. 2/Lieut MC Hartnett reported for duty. Batt Strength 6 off 314 or	
"	16"		In billets. Batt Strength 6 off 312 or	
"	17"		In billets. Batt Strength 6 off 310 or	
LONGPRE	18"	11.30	Batt moved to LONGPRE by Motor Bus. Batt Strength 6 off 310 or	
			Appendix F. Batt Operation Orders No 33	Appendix F
"	19"		In billets. 2/Lt FM West + 2/Lt LT Finan reported for duty. Batt Strength 6 off 310 or	
"	20"		In billets. Batt Strength 6 off 313 or	
VICTORIA	21st	10.21	Batt entrained at LONGPRE. 22	
CAMP.	19.15		Batt detrained at GODEWAERSVELDE and marched to VICTORIA CAMP.	
WESTOUTRE	28.50		B.M. arrived at VICTORIA CAMP. Batt Strength 6 off 312 or	
			Appendix G. Batt Operation order No 34	Appendix G

Army Form C. 2118.

WAR DIARY
or
INTELLIGENCE SUMMARY.
(Erase heading not required.)

1st Royal Munsters   September 1916

Place	Date	Hour	Summary of Events and Information	Remarks and references to Appendices
VICTORIA CAMP	22		In camp. 2/Lieut E C Conley & 2/Lieut P F Martin rejoined. Bn Strength 8 off 312 o.r	
	23		Batt received orders to march to BUTTERFLY FARM.	
		4.00	Batt marched off.	
BUTTERFLY FARM		16.00	Batt arrived BUTTERFLY FARM.	
			Appendix H. Batt Operation order no 25. Batt Strength 10 off 333 o.r.	Appendix H
BUTTERFLY FARM	24		In camp.	
	25		Batt Strength 10 off 351 o.r. Lieut Hartnett posted on leave	
			Batt Strength 9 off 348 o.r. Capt C H Entram Lieut J S Hart & 2/Lt H Delany reported for duty.	
	26		Batt Strength 12 off 325 o.r.	
ROSSIGNOL	27	16.20	Batt marched off from BUTTERFLY FARM.	
		17.45	Batt commenced taking over in line. Appendix I. Batt Operation order.	Appendix I
		20.20	Relief complete. Batt Strength 12 off 325 o.r.	
	28		Line quiet. Batt Strength 12 off 322 o.r.	
			Had quiet. Lost the exception of a few Minnys we fire little or no destroyed from line or tun for duty.	Strength Dairy
	29		Places bld god no other damage. Batt Strength 14 off 321 o.r.	Write Diary
	30		Line quiet. Batt strength 14 off 350 o.r.	Appendix J

R Meurike Major Lieut Col
Comy 1st R Munsters

SECRET   Apendix A   Copy No:- 15

Operation Order No. 31.

By Lieut-Col. R. H. Monck-Mason, Comdg. 1st Royal Munster Fus.

Ref. 1/20,000 Sheet 62.D N.E.

1. The 48th Inf. Brigade will move to F.24 S.W. of BILLON FARM on 3rd September and be in Corps Reserve and ready to move from there at one hour's notice.

2. The Battn. will parade ready to march off at 9-30 a.m. to-morrow.

   Order of march:-

            Snipers,
            Signallers,
            Bombers,
            Runners,

   W. Coy. X Coy. Y Coy. Z Coy. Lewis Gun Detmt.
   O.C. Z Coy. will detail an officer to march in rear with the Police.

   Route:- Tracks from SAND-PIT F.18.d., E.S.E to F.16.c. 3.0., thence in a South Easterly direction to F.29.

3. Supply & Baggage Wagons of Units will march Brigaded under the orders of O.C. 45 Coy. R.S.C., leaving at 11-30 a.m. or as soon as re-filling is completed.

4. ALL 1st Line Transport will accompany Units.

5. All kits to be loaded in Transport lines by 8 a.m.

6. All water bottles will be filled before marching off, and on arrival at destination O.C. Coys. will hold an inspection to see that no water has been consumed en route.

7. Dress:- Field Service Marching Order.

Issued at:- 7-15 p.m.

A. Williams
Capt.
Adjutant 1st Royal Munster Fusiliers

2-9-16

Appendix B

REPORT ON THE PART TAKEN BY THE 1st. ROYAL MUNSTER FUSILIERS ON THE CAPTURE OF GINCHY.

:-:

On the afternoon of the 9th September, 1916, when the barrage fire opened, the Battalion was occupying the line of trenches T.20.a-1.4 to T.19.d.3.3 with the 8th Royal Munster Fusiliers on their right and the 7th Royal Irish Rifles on the left.

At ZERO time (4-45) the Battalion left the trenches in four waves with a platoon front per company, disposed as follows:- 'from right to left X W Y Z With the exception of 2/Lt. Baily all the officers were either killed or wounded within 50 yards of our own trench.

X. Coy. under 2/Lt. Baily pushed forward towards the first objective but finding that the right flank was exposed owing to the fact that the 8th Battn. R. Munster Fus. were being mown down from the left flank by 2 Machine Guns posted about T.20 a ½.8 he wheeled to the right and occupied a position along the trench T.20 a.1.3½ to T.20.a ½.7 where he dug himself in. The first two waves of his company were practically wiped out leaving him with 28 men.

W & Y companies who were both weak to start with and without officers from the commencement became merged in other Units and were carried on in the advance past the first objective.

Z Coy. under Sgt-Major Harris advanced direct on the first objective at about T 19 b.7.8, the platoons on the right were held up by the enemy who were entrenched at this point. Sgt-Major Harris wheeled the left of his company and charged, driving the enemy out. A German officer reorganized the scattered enemy and occupied a trench further to the East. Sgt-Major Harris encircled there on the West and North West and dispersed them with heavy loss. He again advanced and found the enemy strongly entrenched in a position about T 13 d.7.0. He dug in opposite them and with the assistance of of one Machine Gun held his position until relieved.

Owing to the absence of officers and the difficulty of the ground several small parties got separated and joined other Units. Parts of the two centre companies joined the Royal Irish Rifles and 8th Royal Dublin Fus. and eventually went on with the supporting Battalions to the second objective.

The remnants of W & Y Coy. who had been carried forward to the second objective were collected and joined the H.Q. Coy. and assisted the consolidation of the position. One party working on the second line and a party under Sgt. Silva on the right flank.

On my arrival I proceeded to the first objective allotted to my Battalion and finding that all troops had over shot the mark and had been carried through to the second objective, I proceeded straight on but not seeing any of my men I returned to the fist objective and was just sending runners round to ascertain the position of the Battalion when I met Lieut-Col. Bellingham who told me that Lieut-Col. Francis was at the farm at T.3.c.5½.3 where I proceeded. With the assistance of Lieut-Col. Bellingham and Lieut-Col. Francis the position was gone into and a systematic reorganization of the scattered Units started.

Capt. Allen R.E. reported later and gave valuable information as also did the Act.Adjutant 8th R. Dublin Fus.

The units were roughly distributed as follows:- 'One Coy. 8th R. Dublin Fs with a Machine Gun and on their left the remnants of Z coy. 1st. Royal Munster Fus. roughly from T.20.a.0.8 to T.13 b.7.1½. from point (54) to strong point (42). Part of H.Q. Coy. 1st. R. Munster Fus. on the right and 8th R. Dublin Fus. and 7th R. Irish Fus. from point (42) to point T.13 central. 7th R. Irish Fus. 8th Inniskillings, 8th R. Dublin Fus. and 9th R. Dublin Fus.

All the troops that could be collected were turned in to consolidate the first objective consisting of part of H.Q. 1st. R. Munster Fus.

and some men of the Battalion who had gone through with the supporting Battalions and men of other Units who had lost their
Battalions.

The enemy were in some strength in trenches between point 54 and the line held by the company of the 8th R. Dublin Fus. at S 20 a o 8 to T 13 b 7. 1½ forming a constant menace. Furthermore we were unable to obtain contact with the 47th Brigade on our right, but from what one knows now the flank was not in so great danger as was thought at the time, althosugh it was sufficiently serious.

On the left flank connection was gained with the Division on our left after considerable trouble by means of patrols and bombing posts, but this connection was very slender.

At about 10-30 p.m. a Battalion of the Welsh Guards arrived and took over the line from point (42) to T. 13 central and they exended a company along the road leading west from that point.

Owing to the seriousness of the situation I was compelled to retain the relieved troops until further reinforcements arrived, so I kept all the troops that had been relieved on this part of the front in support.

At about 11 a.m. 10th Sept. 1916, a company of the Grenadier Guards arrived and relieved the remainder of the line and the Garrison then marched back to CARNOY.

I cannot speak too highly of the conduct of all the troops both in the attack and in the work of consolidation.

Lieut-Col.

Comdg. 1st. Royal Munster Fusiliers.

SECRET.　　　　　　　　　　　　　　　　　Appendix C.
　　　　　　　　　　　　　　　　　　　　　Copy No. .....

48th Infantry Brigade Operation Order
No. 64.

8. 9. 1916.

Map Reference -
GUILLEMONT Sheet 1/20,000.
and Secret Trench Map 1/10,000.

1.　The following Operation Order cancels the warning order (16th Div.No.E.S. 1226/5, dated 7th instant) already issued as regards dividing line between Brigades, and also as regards any other discrepancies which may be found to exist.

2.(a). The Fourth Army will renew the attack on September 9th at an hour to be notified later.
(b).　XIV Corps is to capture the German position from T.27.b.1.5½. to T.21.d.5½.2½. - point 141.7. (1,000 yards EAST of GINCHY) - the trench along the GINCHY - MORVAL Road to Trench junction T.14.c.5.4½. - T.14.a.4.2, and thence to junction of trenches at T.7.d.4.0.
(c).　XV Corps will carry out a simultaneous operation on left of XIV Corps.

3.(a)　The XIV Corps attack will be carried out by the 56th Division on the Right and the 16th Division on Left.
　　Dividing line between 56th and 16th Divisions will be the line from GUILLEMONT-LEUZE WOOD road at T.20.d.1.5. to trench junction at T.14.d.8½.4. (inclusive to 56th Division).
(b).　Dividing line between 16th Division and 55th Division (XV Corps attack will be T.13.c.6½.1½. - T.13 (central) - trench junction T.7.d.4.0.
(c).　The objectives allotted to 56th Division are as follows :-

First Objective - T.27.b.1.5½. - T.21.d.5½.2½. - T.21.a.8.2½.
　　　　　　　　　T.20.b.4½.3½.

Second Objective - T.21.a.6.2½. - T.15.c.1.4½. - T.14.d.8½.4.

4.　The 16th Division attack will be carried out by the 47th Inf. on Right and 48th Inf. Bde. on Left. Dividing lines between Brigades will be the GINCHY - WEDGEWOOD road from present front line to T.20.a.1.6. (to 48th Inf. Bde.) and thence the trench running to ~~T.14.a.4.2.~~ (to ~~47th~~ Inf. Bde.)
T./4.c.5.4　　48½

5.　The objectives allotted to Brigades are shewn on the attached map "A", together with boundaries between Brigades and with neighbouring Divisions. The objectives allotted to Brigades are as follows : ~~XXXXXXXXXXXXXX~~.
(a). 47th Inf. Bde. First objective T.20.b.4½.3½. - point where trench crosses GINCHY-LEUZE WOOD Road at T.14.c.3½.1½.

　　　　　　　Second objective, trench junction at T.14.d.8½.4 (exclusive).-point where trench crosses road at T.14.c.5.4½. (inclusive).

(b). 48th Infantry Brigade.
First objective - Point where trench crosses GINCHY - LEUZE WOOD road at T.14.c.3½.1½. (exclusive) - road junction T.13.d.7.3½. - T.13.(central).

Second objective - Point where trench crosses road at T.14.c.5.4 (exclusive) - T.14.a.4.2. - trench junction at T.7.d.4.0.

2.

6. (a). H.Q., 47th Inf. Bde. is at present at BRIQUETERIE (A.4.b).
It may however be moved further forward.

(b). Two Companies 11th Hants are placed at the disposal of
47th Inf. Bde. for these operations.

(c). At Zero Time, 47th Inf. Bde. will advance with two Battalions
in front line to their first objective and consolidate.

(d). At Zero plus 40 minutes the remaining two Battalions will
advance to their second objective and consolidate. The two
Companies 11th Hnats will act as directed by G.O.C. 47th Inf.
Bde.

(e). G.O.C., 47th Inf. Bde. will arrange to establish strong
points at T.20.a.8.9. and T.14.c. Central.

7. (a). H.Q., 48th Inf. Bde. will be at DUMMY Trench (S.23.c.8.4.)
(b). At ZERO time, 48th Inf. Bde. will advance with two Battalions
to their first objective and consolidate.
(c). At Zero plus 40 minutes, the remaining two Battalions will
advance to the second objective and consolidate.
(d). G.O.C., 48th Inf. Bde. will arrange for parties to clear
all cellars and dug-outs in GINCHY.
(e). He will also arrange to establish strong points at T.14.a 4.2
at the Northern corner of GINCHY and at T.7.d.4.0.

8. 49th Inf. Bde. will relieve the garrison of GUILLEMONT on
night 8/9th September. Relief to be completed by 5.0 A.M. by
which hour 49th Inf. Bde. will be in position as follows :-
(a). H.Q. - BERNAFAY WOOD (S.28.b. central).
(b). 1 Batt. - In new trenches at N.E. corner of GUILLEMONT.
(c). 1 Batt. - In GUILLEMONT. This Battalion will move to and
occupy trenches east of GUILLEMONT from road junction
T.20.c.1.4. to T.20.a.1.1. as soon as these trenches are
vacated by 47th Inf. Bde.
(d). Remaining two Battalions will occupy the old British line
from ARROW HEAD COPSE (S.30.b.3.2.) to the GRIDIRON
(T.19.a.3.7.)

9. Observation on to the ORVAL - LESBOEUFS line is a <u>necessity</u>.
Infantry Brigades, therefore, on reaching their objectives will
once push forward patrols and establish posts from which this
information can be obtained.

10. 155th and 156th Field Companies are placed at disposal of 47th
and 48th Inf. Bdes. respectively. Representatives of these
Companies will report to Infantry Brigadiers for instruction on
receipt of these orders.

11. On relief by 49th Inf. Bde. in GUILLEMONT, the 11th Hants
(less 2 Coys.) placed at disposal of 47th Inf. Bde.) and 157th Fd.
Company will proceed to BERNAFAY WOOD, where they will be held in
Divisional Reserve. On arrival, they will report their new
positions with map references and will each send two orderlies
who know these positions to report to O.C. 16th Div. Sig. Coy.
at Divisional Headquarters.

12. The attack will be preceded by a deliberate Heavy Artillery
bombardment commencing at 7.0 A.M. and continuing until Zero
time with an interval from 11.20 A.M. to 11.50 A.M. for
photography.
During this bombardment certain trenches may have to be
cleared from time to time. Instructions as to this will be sent
later to those concerned.

12. (b). The Field Artillery supporting 16th Division will be organised in two groups as follows :-

Right Group.
Lieut. Col. McCARTHEY, C.M.G.) To support 47th Inf. Bde.)

Left Group.
Lieut. Col. BUZZARD)   To support 48th Inf. Bde.

(c). Fifty per cent of the Field Artillery guns covering the Division will be employed for stationary barrage and fifty per cent for creeping barrage.

The creeping barrage will in all cases advance at the rate of 50 yards per minute in front of the Infantry. When the creeping barrage reaches the stationary barrage the stationary barrage will lift on to the next barrage line.

(d). At zero, when the Infantry advance to their first objective, an intense Field Artillery barrage will open.

(e). At zero plus 40 minutes, when the Infantry advance to their second objective, the barrage will again become intense.

(f). The above barrages are shewn on the attached Map A.

13. DISPOSITION OF UNITS.

On the morning of the Assault, the troops of the Brigade will be formed up in trenches as follows :-
1st R. Munster Fusiliers with their Right flank on T.20.a.1.3. and their Left on T.19.b.3.5., in touch with 8th Muns., 44th Inf. Bde.
The 7th R. Irish Rifles with their Right on T.19.b.2.6. and their Left on T.13.c.4.3., in touch with 2/5th Lancs. Fusiliers, 164th Infantry Brigade.
The 8th Dublins will hold the trenches immediately in rear of the 1st R. Munster Fusiliers.
The 9th Dublins will hold the trenches immediately in rear of the 7th R. Irish Rifles.

6 guns, 48th Machine Gun Company will be in/position at the following points :-

from which they will co-operate with the bombardment and the Assault.
The hour and full details as to the Route each Unit is to move by will be issued later.

14. (a). 1st PHASE.
The Assault will be delivered by two Battalions, 1st R. Munster Fusiliers on the Right and the 7th Royal Irish Rifles on the Left.
To these Battalions is allotted the task of capturing the first objective (coloured RED on Map "A".)
The divining between these two Battalions is the GUILLEMONT - GINCHY Road, as far as the first objective (inclusive to Right Battalion).
Each Battalion will assault with four compnaies in the Front line, in depth, on a front of one platoon per company, platoons to be at not less than 40 yards distance.
At -05, the Assaulting Battalions will, if circumstances permit, commence filing out of the trenches, the leading two waves being out by Zero hour; the remainder will follow at ZERO.
At ZERO hour these two Battalions will advance over the open and move straight on to the first objective (coloured RED in Map "A".), following in the wake of the Artillery barrage.
The three leading waves of the assaulting troops will not delay their advance for slight opposition, or for the purpose of

clearing up trenches and dug-outs; these will be dealt with by the fourth waves - Bombers will be told off to deal with these cellars.

On reaching the first objective, the assaulting Battalions will commence to consolidate this line, and establish a strong point at T.13.d.7.3.

The O.C. 156th Field Company R.E. will detail 1 Section to assist in this work. This party will follow in rear of the fourth waves. To each of these Battalions will be allotted 1 Section of Stokes Guns. Owing to the difficulty in supplying ammunition, these guns should be used for defences purposes when the objective has been reached. These guns will follow in rear of the fourth waves.

(b). 2nd PHASE.

At ZERO plus 40, the remaining two Battalions, 8th Royal Dublin Fusiliers on the Right and 9th Royal Dublin Fusiliers on the Left will advance to the second objective and consolidate.

The dividing line between Battalions will be the GUILLEMONT GINCHY as far as first objective, thence to point T.14.a.2½.4½.

The formation to be adopted will be as for the 1st PHASE of the attack mentioned in para. 14 (a).

The strong points to be consolidated will be:-
T.7.d.4.0. and T.14.a.4.2.

The O.C., 156th Fd. Co. R.E. will detail two Sections to assist in this work. These Sections will follow in rear of the fourth waves.

Bombers will be told off to deal with cellars.

XX. To each of these two Battalions will be allotted 1 Section 48th M.G. Company. This will follow in rear of the fourth wave and will assist in the consolidation of the second objective.

15. As the fourth wave of the Assault of the second Phase passes the first objective, the two sections of the 48th T. Battery will go forward and assist in the consolidation of the second objective.

16. The remaining guns of the 48th M.G. Company and T.M. Battery will remain in Reserve at the QUARRY T.19.c.1.3.

17. No. 9 Squadron R.F.C. will have two contact aeroplanes in the air from ZERO to ZERO plus two hours, After that one contact aero until dark, and one from 5.30 A.M. to 8.0 A.M. on 10th Sept.
Flares will be lit as follows :-
(a). On obtaining each objective.
(b). At 6.30 P.M. on Sept 9th.
(c). At 6.0 A.M. on Sept. 10th.

18. Watches will be synchronised at 6.15 P.M. on Sept. 8th and at 9.15 A.M. on Sept 9th.

19. All prisoners are to be sent to the ADVANCED PRISONERS OF WAR POST on the MONTAUBAN - CARNOY Road at the Craters (A.8.a.8.4.) where they will be searched under arrangements to be made by the A.P.M., 16th Division. Receipts will be given for prisoners and escorts will then return to their units.

20. The following equipment, Ammunition, Bombs, etc., will be carried by each Infantry Soldier :-
Rifle - Equipment including water-proof sheet but without pack or greatcoat.

Haversacks to be carried on the back.
Water-bottles full.
Two bandoliers of ammunition in addition to equipment ammunition.
Iron Rations and the unexpended portion of the day's rations.
Two bombs.
Two sandbags.
Flares for signalling to aeroplanes on the scale of 1 to every 2 men if available.

21. A dump of 20 boxes of emergency rations and water will be made on the eastern side of THRONES WOOD at S.30.a.3.8. These will not be used except in the greatest emergency.

Dumps for S.A.A. are at the Western edge of BERANFAY WOOD and will be established on the east side of THRONES WOOD about S.30.a.3.8. and also at S.30.a.4.3.

22. SANDBAGS. will be drawn from R.E. Dump at Western edge of BERNAFAY WOOD.

TOOLS - A dump of Tools will be established at the N.W. corner of BERNAFAY WOOD ~~S.30.a.3.8.~~ ~~and at~~

23. MEDICAL ARRANGEMENTS. The Advanced Bearer Post is at BERNAFAY WOOD. S.23.c.1.1½.
Advanced Dressing Station at CARNOY - A.13.d.3.8.

24. The Brigade Signalling Officer, *will arrange* for Post Offices to be established at T.19.c.1½.3½. and at CORNISH ALLEY, about S.24.b. Central and for an Advanced Report Centre, if possible, in the first objective at GINCHY, about T.13.d.7.3. and in the second objective about T.14.a.4.2.
A Lamp Signal Receiving Station will be extablished at S.24.a.2.0.

25. Until the first objective is gained, the Headquarters of all four Battalions will be in trench T.19A.5.0. to T.19.a.7.2.

26. MESSAGE TO THE TROOPS.

The G.O.C. wishes all ranks "Good luck". He has every confidence that they will carry out the task allotted to them with the courage and determination characteristic of the Irish race.

27. ACKNOWLEDGE.

C. Ald. Alexander

Captain,
Brigade Major, 48th Infantry Brigade.

Issued at 6.0 P.M.

Copy No. 1 and 2 War Diary.
3 Filed.
4 G.O.C.
5 7th Irish Rifles.
6 1st Munsters.
7 8th Dublins.
8 9th Dublins.
9 48th M.G. Company.
10 48th T.M. Battery.
11 Brigade Signals.
12 Staff Captain.
13 16th Division.
14 16th Division "Q".
15 A.D.M.S. 16th Division.
16 C.R.E. 16th Division.
17 155th Fd. Co. R.E.
18 156th Fd. Co. R.E.
19 157th Fd. Co. R.E.
20 47th Inf. Bde.
21 49th Inf. Bde.
22 164th Inf. Bde.
23 11th Hants Pioneers.
24 Guards Div. Artillery.
25 6th Div. Artillery.

SECRET Appendix D

OPERATION ORDER No.31A.

By Lieut-Col. R.H. Monck-Mason, Comdg. 1st. Royal Munster Fusiliers.

Map reference. Guillemont Sheet 1/20,000.

1. The 4th Army will renew the attack to-morrow Sept. 9th.

2. The 48th Brigade 16th Division will attack first objective T 14 c 3½ 1½ (exclusive) to T 13 d 7.3 to T 13 (central).
   Second objective T 14 c 5.4 to T 14 a 4.2 to T 7 d 4.0.

3. The H.Q. 48th Brigade will be at DUMMY TRENCH (S 23 c. 8.4)

4. 1st. Royal Munster Fusiliers will attack from their present line.

5. The attack will be preceeded by a heavy bombardment commencing at 7 a.m. and continuing until Zero time with an interval from 11-20 a.m to 11-50 a.m for photography.

6. The creeping barrage will in all cases advance at the rate of 50 yards per minute in front of the infantry.

7. The assault will be delivered by two Battalions, 1st. R.M.F. on the right, 7th R.I.R. on the left.
   The two Battalions will capture first objective and consolidate.
   The dividing line between Battalions will be the GUILLEMONT-GINCHY Road (inclusive) to right Battn.

8. The 1st. Royal Munster Fusiliers will assault with four companies in front line in depth on a front of one platoon per company. Platoons to be not less than 40 yards distance. The leading platoon will crawl out at 05 and the advance will commence at Zero and move straight to the first objective in the wake of the artillery barrage.
   Companies will be in position right and left X Y W Z.
   The three leading waves will lead straight on to the first objective, the fourth will clear up dug-outs and trenches.

9. The objective for the 1st. Royal Munster Fus. will be T 14 c.3.1. (exclusive) to T 13 d 7.3.

10. 2nd Phase at Zero plus 40 the remaining two Battalions 8th R.D.F. on the right and 9th R.D.F. on the left will advance to the second objective and consolidate.

11. One Section 48th M.G. Coy. will be attached to Z Coy. to consolidate strong point.

12. Watches to be synchronised at 7 a.m and 9-15 a.m on Sept. 9th.

13. All prisoners will be sent to MONTAUBAN.

14. Battle order will be worn, water bottles to be full. Two bandoliers of ammunition in addition to equipment ammunition per man also iron ration and unexpended portion of day's ration, two bombs and two sand bags.

15. Until the first objective is gained Battn. H.Q. will be in trenches at T 19 a 6.1.

(signed) R.H. Monck-Mason, Lieut-Col.
8-9-16. Comdg. 1st. Royal Munster Fusiliers.

SECRET.

OPERATION ORDER No.

SECRET.   Appendix E

OPERATION ORDER No.32.

By Lieut-Col. R.H. Monck-Mason, Comdg. 1st. Royal Munster Fusiliers.

1. The 48th Inf. Brigade will move into rest billets in CORBIE to-day.

2. The Battalion will parade facing S. ready to march off at 12-30 p.m. in the following order "W X" "Y Z" and H.Q. Company.
   W & X will form one company, Y & Z another. Dress:- Battle order.
   Route:- Tracks to L.1.a.6.1.-K.6.d-K.11.a. MORLANCOURT-CROSS ROADS K.20.b. Main Road to Corbie.

3. There will be a halt for two hours at 2 p.m for dinners at K.9.b. just East of MORLANCOURT. The march will be resumed at 4 p.m. The Cook.Sgt. will arrange to cook dinners for the 48th T.M. Batt.

4. The 1st. Line Transport will march brigaded under Bde.Transport Off. Transport must rejoin Battalion at the halting place East of MORLANCOURT.

5. O.C. Y Z. Coy. will detail a good N.C.O. to march in rear of the Battn. and bring along stragglers.

                                        (signed) J.H.C. Lawlor 2/Lieutp
11-9-16.   A.F/Adjutant 1st. R. M. F.

SECRET.

Appendix F

OPERATION ORDER No.33.

By Lieut-Col. R.H. Monck-Mason, Comdg. 1st. Royal Munster Fusiliers.

1. The 48th Brigade will move to-morrow by motor bus and on arrival at destination fill be temporarily attached to 10th Corps.

2. Busses will be drawn up on the LANEUVILLE – 'VECQUEMONT Road facing West at 11-30 a.m.

3. The Battalion will parade on the rad outside Orderly Room at 9-45 a.m ready to march off in the following order:-
   H.Q. Company
   Z   "
   Y   "
   X   Z
   W   "

   Busses are allotted as follows:-
   No.1. C.O. Adjutant Quartermaster Padre Interpreter M.O. 2/Lt. Baily 2/Lt. M.C. Hartnett and Officers Mess.
   No.2.3.4.5. Headquarter Coy. Sgt-Major, Coy.Qrmr Sgts. Orderly Room, 2 H.Q. Orderlies will travel on No. 2 Buss.
   No.6.7p8. Z Company.   No.9.10.11 Y. Coy.
   12.13.14 X. Coy. 15.16.17. W. Coy.
   Coy. sgt-Majors will aportion their men accordingly.
   The Provost Sgt and 4 Police will travel on No.17 Bus.

4. Lieut. T.H. Poingdestre and 2/Lt. R.M. Hall are detailed to travel on the last bus. and see all busses are properly loaded.

5. All billets will be thoroughly cleaned before leaving.

                                        (signed) J.H.C. Lawlor 2/Lieut.
17-9-16.   A/Adjutant 1st. Royal Munster Fus.

SECRET.   Appendix G

OPERATION ORDER No.34.

By Lieut-Col. R.H. Monck-Mason, Comdg. 1st. Royal Munster Fusiliers.

1. The 48th Brigade will entrain at LONGPRE on 21st inst.

2. The Battalion will parade ready to march off at 8-15 a.m. on the road outside the church in the following order:-
   - W. Coy.
   - X "
   - Y "
   - Z "
   - H.Q. "
   - Lewis Gunners.

3. The Transport will entrain with the Battalion and report to R.T.O. at 6-45 a.m. The T.M. Detachment will parade with the Transport. Transport Officer has been given instructions for entraining.

4. 2/Lt. R.M. Hall and 29 men from Z. Coy. will report to the R.T.O. at 5-45 a.m. to assist in loading vehicles etc.

5. A billeting party of one N.C.O. per company and the Interpreter under the orders of 2/Lt. C.T. Fraser will report to the Adjutant 7th Royal Irish Rifles at LONGPRE Station at 12 midnight, 20/21st. and travel on the first train.

6. The R.T.O. is responsible for loading trains and all his orders will be carried out and every assistance given him.

(signed) J.H.C. Lawlor 2/Lieut.

20-9-16.   A/Adjutant 1st. R. Munster Fus.

SECRET.   Appendix H   Copy No. 14

Operation Order No. 35.

By Lieut-Col. R.H. Monck-Mason, Comdg. 1st Royal Munster Fusiliers

Reference BELGIUM & FRANCE
sheet No. 28 S.W. 1/20,000.

1. The 118th Inf. Brigade will relieve the 73rd CANADIAN BATTN. in the LEFT SECTOR (VIERSTRATT) on the 23rd September and night of 23/24th Sept.

2. The Battalion will be in Brigade Reserve at BUTTERFLY FARM – N.19.a.6.9.

3. The Battalion will parade ready to march off at 2 p.m 23rd Sept.   Order of march:-
   - Snipers
   - Pioneers
   - Bombers
   - Signallers
   - Runners
   - W Coy.
   - X "
   - Y "
   - Z "
   - Lewis Guns
   - Police

   Z Coy. will detail one officer to be in charge of the Police.
   The Battalion will march by companies at 300 yards interval East of a North and South line running through BRULOOZE.
   Dress:- Marching Order.

4. The Battn. Transport Lines will be at M.23.c.7.6

5. Brigade H.Q will be at BRULOOZE (M.18.d.6.2.)

                                        A. Cowley, 2/Lieut
                                        a/Adjutant 1st R.M.F.

23-9-16

SECRET Appendix I Copy No:- 1

Operation Order No:- 36

By Lieut-Col. R. H. Monck-Mason, Comdg. 1st R. Munster Fus.

Ref. sheet 28 S.W. 1/20,000

1. 1st R.M.F. will relieve the 7th R.I.R. in the LEFT SUB-SECTION J 2. [N 24.a.5.3] [exclusive] to K1 N 18.C.4.0. [inclusive] and will also take over STRONG POINTS:- TURNERSTOWN RIGHT. S.P. 13 OLD. TURNERSTOWN LEFT. FORT HALIFAX. FORT MOUNT ROYAL on Sept. 27th. Battalion H.Q. will be at ROSSIGNOL N.22.a.8.4.

2. The Battalion will march off at 5 p.m. with intervals of 300 yards between Companies. Order of March:-
   W. Coy.   X. Coy.   Y. Coy.   Z. Coy.
   Lewis Guns
   H.Q. Coy.

3. Position of companies:- W Coy. front line J 2 [exclusive] to K1 [inclusive]. X. Coy. TURNERSTOWN RIGHT.

   Y. Coy { S.P. 13 OLD.
          { TURNERSTOWN LEFT

   Z. Coy { FORT HALIFAX
          { FORT MOUNT ROYAL

4. Guides will meet Companies at the Church KEMMEL.

5. Completion of relief to be immediately reported to Battn. H.Q. by wire.

Issued at:- 3.50 p.m.
27-9-16

J. Conly 2/Lieut
A/Adjutant 1st R.M.F.

Appendix J

STRENGTH DIARY.

Strength Sept.1st. 37 Offs. 739 O.R. Draft ow 14 O.R. To. Hosp. 1 O.R.
                              Sept. 2nd.
Strength 37 Offs. 752 O.R.   To Hosp. 2 O.R.
                              Sept. 3rd.
Strength 37 Offs. 750 O.R.
                              Sept.4th.
Strength 37 Offs. 750 O.R. Wounded 8 Offs. 13 O.R. Missing 2 O.R.
                              Killed 3 O.R. To Hosp. 1 Off. 4 O.R.
                              Sept. 5th.
Strength 28 Offs. 728 O.R. 5 Offs. joined Killed 7 O.R. Wounded 14 O.R.
                              To Hosp. 4 O.R.
                              Sept. 6th.
Strength 33 Offs. 703 O.R. Killed 2 Offs. 6 O.R. Wounded 15 O.R.
                              Missing 1 Off 2 O.R.
                              Sept. 7th.
Strength 30 Offs 680 O.R. Wounded 1 Off. 8 O.R. Missing 1 O.R.
                              To Hosp. 33 O.R.
                              Sept. 8th.
Strength 28 Offs. 638 O.R. Joined 1 Off. 5 O.R. Wounded 10 O.R.
                              To Hosp. 5 O.R. Killed 2 O.R. Missing 3 O.R.
                              Sept. 9th.
Strength 29 Off. 623 O.R. Killed 5 Offs. 33 O.R. Missing 1 Off. 53 O.R.
                              Wounded 6 Offs. 106 O.R. To Hosp. 18 O.R.
                              Sept. 10th.
Strength 17 Offs. 413 O.R.
                              Sept.11th.
Strength 17 Offs. 413 O.R. Wounded 3 O.R. To Hosp. 1 O.R.
                              Sept. 12th.
Strength 17 Offs. 409 O.R.   To Hosp. 1 O.R.
                              Sept. 13th.
Strength 17 Offs. 409 O.R.   To Hosp. 1 O.R.
                              Sept. 14th.
Strength 17 Offs. 408 O.R. To Hosp. 2 O.R. Reinforcements 14 O.R.
                              Sept. 15th.
Strength 17 Offs. 420 O.R. To Hosp. 2 O.R. 1 Off. rejoined from Hosp.
                              Sept.16th.
Strength 17 Offs. 418 O.R. To Hosp. 4 O.R. rejoined 2 O.R.
                              Sept. 17th.
Strength 17 O.R. 416 O.R.
                              Sept. 18th.
Strength 17 Offs. 416 O.R.
                              Sept. 19th.
Strength 17 Offs. 416 O.R. 2 Offs. joined.   3 O.R. joined.
                              Sept. 20th.
Strength 19 Offs. 419 O.R.   To Hosp. 1 O.R.
                              Sept. 21st.
Strength 19 Offs. 418 O.R.
                              Sept. 22nd.
Strength 19 Offs. 418 O.R.   Draft of 31 O.R.
                              Sept. 23rd.
Strength 19 Offs. 449 O.R. To Hosp. 1 O.R.
                              Sept. 24th.
Strength 19 Offs. 448 O.R.   To Hosp. 2 O.R.

	Sept. 25th.
Strength 19 Offs. 450 O.R.	Struck off 14 O.R. To Hosp. 7 O.R.
	Sept. 26th.
Strength 19 Offs. 429 O.R.	To Hosp. 3 O.R. 3 Offs. joined
	Sept. 27th.
Strength 22 Offs. 426 O.R.	
	Sept. 28th.
Strength 22 Offs. 426 O.R.	To Hosp. 1 O.R. 2 Offs. joined.
	Sept. 29th.
Strength 24 Offs. 426 O.R.	1 O.R. to Hosp. Draft 30 O.R.
	Sept. 30th.
Strength 24 Offs. 456 O.R.	1 O.R. to Hospital.

WAR DIARY

MONTH OF OCTOBER, 1916.

VOLUME

1st Munster Fusiliers

Army Form C. 2118.

WAR DIARY
or
INTELLIGENCE SUMMARY.

OCTOBER 1916 1st Royal Munster Fusiliers

(Erase heading not required.)

Instructions regarding War Diaries and Intelligence Summaries are contained in F.S. Regs., Part II. and the Staff Manual respectively. Title pages will be prepared in manuscript.

Place	Date	Hour	Summary of Events and Information	Remarks and references to Appendices
In the Trenches	1st		Left Subsection. Line Quiet. Lieut L.H. CARRIGAN reported for duty from 3rd RMF. Appendix A. Bde Op.Ord. 30/9/16. Appendix B. Batt. Op. Ord. 37.	App A & B
"	2nd		Line Quiet. 2nd Lts B.S. CUMMING & R.W. MARSHALL reported for duty from 3rd RMF on first appointment.	App C
"	3rd		Line Quiet.	
"	4th		Line Quiet.	
KLONDYKE FARM	5th		Battalion relieved in the front line by 7th Bn Irish Rifles and moved into Brigade Support.	
		3 pm	Relief commenced	
		5 pm	Relief completed. Appendix D. Batt. Op. Ord. 39.	App D
"	6th		In billets & huts	
"	7th		" "	
"	8th		" " Lieut Col. A.W. CLERKE reported for duty as 2 in Command from 3rd RMF.	
"	9th		" "	
"	10th		" "	
"	11th		" "	
"	12th		" " Brev Lt Col R. Monck-Mason took over the duties of Acting Brigadier 48 Bde. Lieut Col. A.W. Clerke took over the duties of OC. 1st RMF.	
"	13th		Battalion relieved 7th R. Irish Rifles in the front line	

WAR DIARY or INTELLIGENCE SUMMARY

Army Form C. 2118.

OCTOBER 1916 — 1st Royal Munster Fus.

Place	Date	Hour	Summary of Events and Information	Remarks and references to Appendices
	13	2.30 pm	Relief Commenced	Appendix E See Orders
	"	4.30 pm	Relief Completed	2nd Lieut W.D.W.Kennaw reported for duty from 3 Reserve Regt. Capt R.H. Bonsall – Eye Strain Kd of Batt.
	14		Line quiet	
	15		Line quiet	
	16		Line quiet	
	17		Enemy active all day. Relief took place of Coy group in front line, which was left to the Coys O.C.C	Hd line
	18		Line quiet	
	19		Line quiet	
	20		Line quiet	
LOCRE	21		Battalion relieved in the front line by 7 Royal Irish Rifles & moved into Billets Divisional Reserve at LOCRE	
	"	2 pm	Relief Commenced	Appendix F. O'Orders No 4/1 appendix G. Bn.Orders No 77 appx F + g
	"	4 pm	Relief Completed	
	22		In Billets + huts	
	23		" " "	
	24		" " "	

Army Form C. 2118.

WAR DIARY OCTOBER 1916
or
INTELLIGENCE SUMMARY.
1st Royal Munster Fus.

(Erase heading not required.)

Instructions regarding War Diaries and Intelligence Summaries are contained in F. S. Regs., Part II. and the Staff Manual respectively. Title pages will be prepared in manuscript.

Place	Date	Hour	Summary of Events and Information	Remarks and references to Appendices
	25th		In Billets + Huts. Lieut. E.J. MAHONEY reported for duty	
	26th		" Lieut. J.G. MATTERSON + Lieut. J.R. BALDWIN. 2nd Lieut. H.E.N. FARRELL	
			" 2nd Lieut. J.H. HARTLEY reported for duty, 2nd Lieut. R.M. HALL Struck off Strength	
	27th		" Lieut. D.T. HALL, 2nd Lieut. J.A. FISHER Struck off the strength of Batt	
	28th		" Line quiet.	
	29th		" Battalion relieved the 1st R. I. Rifles in front line. Approaches H.Bge Op green no 76 Opposite Grandcourt. J. Batt Op order no 42	App "H + J"
Near dn	30th		Line quiet	
	31st		" "	

SECRET.

Ref. 28.S.W. OPERATION ORDER No. 37.

Appendix B

By Lieut-Col. S.U. Monck-Mason, Comdg. 1st. Royal Munster Fusiliers.

1. The Battalion will be relieved in the front line from N.24.a.4½.8. to N.18.c.4.0. TURNERSTOWN LEFT S.P. 13 OLD and K 1.A. to-night 30th September. Half X Coy. in TURNERSTOWN LEFT will on relief move to TURNERSTOWN RIGHT.
Y. Coy. in S.P. 13 OLD and K 1.A. will on relief move to FORT HALIFAX and relieve half Z Coy.
Half Z Coy. on relief in FORT HALIFAX will move to FORT MOUNT ROYAL.
Completion of relief must be immediately wired to Battalion H.Q.
Handing over certificates to be sent to Battn. H.Q. by 9 a.m Oct. 1st.

All watches will be put back one hour at 1a.m. Oct. 1st., hours for "stand to" will be revised accordingly.

(signed) E.C. Conley 2/Lieut.

30.9.16.   A/Adjutant 1st. Royal Munster Fusiliers.

Strength   Oct. 1st.
24 Offs. 452 O.R.   Capt. Carrigan arrived. 1 O.R. wounded.
                                 Oct. 2nd.
25 Offs. 451 O.R.   2/Lieuts. Marshall & Cuming arrived. Reinforcements 10.
                                 Oct. 3rd.
27 Offs. 461 O.R.   2/Lt. J.R. Howe struck off. To hosp. 1 O.R.
                                 Oct. 4th
26 Offs. 460 O.R.
                                 Oct. 4th.
26 Offs. 460 O.R.
                                 Oct. 5th.
26 Offs. 460 O.R.   1 O.R. killed. 1 O.R. to Hosp.
                                 Oct. 6th.
26 Offs. 458 O.R.
                                 Oct. 7th.
26 Offs. 458 O.R.   To Hosp. 2 O.R.
                                 Oct. 8th.
26 Offs. 456 O.R.   Lieut-Col. Clarke D.S.O. arrived. 1 O.R. rejoined.
                                 Oct. 9th.
27 Offs. 457 O.R..   Reinforcements 28 O.R. Capt. Quare struck off
                                 To Hosp. 2 O.R.
                                 Oct. 10th.
26 Offs. 483 O.R.   4 O.R. rejoined.
                                 Oct. 11th.
26 Offs. 487 O.R.   Reinforcements 12. From Hosp. 2 O.R. 1 O.R. Wounded
                                 1 O.R. to Hosp.
                                 Oct. 12th.
26 Offs. 497 O.R.   To Hosp. 5 O.R.
                                 Oct. 13th.
26 Offs. 492 O.R.   2/Lt. W.D. McKeown arrived. To Hosp. 3 O.R.
                                 Oct. 14th.
27 Offs. 489 O.R.   Capt. R.H. Maunsell-Eyre struck off.
                                 Oct. 15th.
26 Offs. 489 O.R.   To Hosp. 2 O.R.
                                 Oct. 16th.
26 Offs. 487 O.R.   Reinforcements 5. O.R. rejoined 2 O.R. Wounded 3 O.R.
                                 To Hosp. 2 O.R.
                                 Oct. 17th.
26 Offs. 489 O.R.   Killed 2 O.R. Wounded 10 O.R. to Hosp. 4 O.R.
                                 Oct. 18th.
26 Offs. 473 O.R.   Rejoined 2 O.R.   Wounded 3 O.R.
                                 Oct. 19th.
26 Offs. 472 O.R.   Rejoined 2 O.R.   Killed 1 o.r. Wounded 2 o.r.
                                 To Hosp. 2 o.r.
                                 Oct. 20th.
26 Offs. 469 O.R.   To Hosp. 1 o.r.
                                 Oct. 21st.
26 Offs. 468 o.r.   Wounded 1 o.r.
                                 Oct. 22nd.
26 Offs. 467 o.r.   Reinforcements 5 o.r.
                                 Oct. 23rd.
26 Offs. 472 o.r.   Rejoined 1 o.r. To Hosp. 2 o.r.
                                 Oct. 24th.
26 Offs. 471 o.r.   Rejoined 2 o.r.   To Hosp. 1 o.r.
                                 Oct. 25th
26 Offs. 472 o.r.   Rejoined 2 o.r. Lieut. E.J. Mahoney arrived.
                                 Oct. 26th.
27 Offs. 474 O.R.   Lieut. I.G. Watterson, Lieut. G.R. Baldwin,
                     2/Lt. H.E.V. Farrell & 2/Lt. J.H. Hartley arrived.
                     Rejoined 2 O.R. Reinforcements 8 o.r.
                     2/Lieut. R.M. Hall struck off.

Strength   Oct. 27th
30 Offs. 484 O.R. Lieut. D.P. Hall & 2/Lt. J.A. Fisher struck off.
                            To Hosp. 1 o.r.
                    Oct. 28th.
28 Offs. 483 O.R.

                    Oct. 29th.
28 Offs. 483 o.r.   Wounded 3 o.r.
                    Oct. 30th.
28 Offs. 480 o.r.   Rejoined 1 o.r.
                    Oct. 31st.
28 Offs. 481 o.r.   Killed 1 o.r.

Appendix C

S E C R E T.

OPERATION ORDER No.38.

By Lieut-Col. R.H. Monck-Mason, Comdg. 1st. Royal Munster Fusiliers.

1. "X" Coy. will relieve "W" Coy. in the front line.
   Relief commences at 4 p.m. Oct. 1st. On being relieved "W" Coy. will move to TURNERSTOWN RIGHT.

2. Completion of relief will be wired to Battan. H.Q.

(signed) E.C. Comley 2/Lieut.

1-10-16.   A/Adjutant 1st. R. Munster Fusiliers.

SECRET.   Appendix D   Copy No:- 13

Operation Order No: 39

By Lieut-Col. R. H. Monck-Mason, Comdg. 1st R. Munster Fus.

Ref. Sheet 28 S.W 1/20,000

1. The 1st R.M.F. will be relieved in the Left Sub-Section by the 7th R.I.R. on 5th Oct.
   On relief the 1st R.M.F. will move into Brigade Reserve and be disposed as follows:- Battn. H.Q and W & X Coys KLONDYKE FARM, M 24. d.9.4. Y & Z Coys ROSSIGNOL WOOD N 22. a. Central.
   Relief will commence at 3 p.m.
   W.X.Y.Z Companies will provide guides to meet relieving companies at advanced Battn. H.Q. at 3 p.m.

2. Movements East of N 20. d. will be by platoons at 200 yards interval.

3. All permanent working parties and schemes of work will be handed over on relief.

4. Handing over Certificates to be rendered to Battn. H.Q. by 12 noon 6th Oct.

5. Completion of reliefs to be immediately reported to Battn. H.Q. in code by wire.

Issued at :- 5-45 p.m
4-10-16

                                          [signature]
                                          2/Lieut
                                          A/Adjutant 1st R.M.F.

SECRET.   Appendix A.

Operation Order No: 40
By Lieut-Col. A.W. Clarke, D.S.O., Comdg. 1st R. Munster Fusiliers

Reference Map 28 S.W.

1. The 1st Royal Munster Fusiliers will relieve the 7th Royal Irish Rifles in the Left Sub-Section to-morrow 13th October.
   W & X Coys. will relieve the two companies of the 7th R.I.R. in the front line. W Coy. on the right X Coy on the left.
   Y Coy. will relieve the garrisons of TURNERSTOWN RIGHT and FORT MOUNT ROYAL, and have 3 platoons in TURNERSTOWN RIGHT and 1 platoon in FORT MOUNT ROYAL.
   Z Coy. will relieve the garrison of S.P.12.
   W. X. Y & Z Coys. will march off at 2-30 p.m.
   Lewis Gunners will march off at 1-30 p.m.
   H.Q. Coy. will march off at 2-45 p.m.
   1 officer and 1 N.C.O. per company will leave to take over trench stores at 1 p.m.

2. Movements East of N.20.d. will be by platoons at 200 yards interval.

3. All permanent working parties, control posts and schemes of work will be handed over on relief.

4. Standing over certificates to be rendered to Battn. H.Q. by 10 a.m. 14th October.

5. Completion of reliefs to be reported immediately to Battn. H.Q. in code by wire.

Issued at:-   2/Lieut
12-10-16   Adjutant 1st R.M.F.

SECRET   Appendix F   Copy No:-

Operation Order No. 41

By Lieut-Col. H.W. Clarke D.S.O. Comdg. 1st R. Munster Fus.

———)(———

1. The 1st Royal Munster Fusiliers will be relieved in the Left Sub-Section by the 7th Royal Irish Rifles on 21st Oct. 1916.

   On relief the 1st R. Munster Fusiliers will move into billets in LOCRE and will be in Divisional Reserve ready to move at 4 hours notice.

   Billeting party consisting of 2/Lieut. F. M. West, C.S.M. Reaney, 1 N.C.O. and 1 man per company and one man from H.Q. Company will report at Battn. H.Q. at 10 a.m. for orders.

   Relief will commence at 2 p.m.

2. Movements East of N.20.d will be by platoons at 200 yards interval.

3. All permanent working parties and schemes of work will be handed over on relief.

4. Handing over Certificates to be rendered to Battn. H.Q. by 10 a.m. 22nd October.

5. Completion of relief to be immediately notified to Battn. H.Q. in Code by wire.

6. The Transport Officer will arrange for three limbers to be at ROSSIGNOL ESTAMINET by 6-30 p.m. for transport of baggage, and also arrange for removal of water carts. Officers horses to be at 49th I.B. H.Q. at 4 p.m.

7. Company Commanders will report to Battn. H.Q. immediately their companies are in billets.

Reference sheet 28 S.W. 1/20,000

Issued at:-
20-10-16

E. Cunliffe
2/Lieut
A/Adjutant 1st R. Munster Fusiliers

SECRET   Appendix X I

Operation Order No: 42
By Lieut-Col. A. W. Clarke D.S.O. Comdg 1st R. Munster Fus.

Ref sheet 28 S.W 1/20,000

1. The 1st Royal Munster Fusiliers will relieve the 7th Royal Irish Rifles in the Left Sub-Section on 29th October, 1916.

   "X" Company will relieve the right company in the front line.

   "W" Company will relieve the left company in the front line.

   "Y" Company will relieve the Garrison of S.P. 12.

   "Z" Company will relieve the Garrisons of TURNERSTOWN RIGHT and FORT MOUNT ROYAL.

   Advance parties of 1 officer & 1 N.C.O. per company, Sgt. Murphy and 1 man from Lewis Guns, C.S.M. Kenny, and Sgt. Kelly for H.Q. Company will leave at 12 noon to take over trench stores.

   The Battalion will march off by companies at 200 yard interval in the following order:- W. X. Y. Z. H.Q. Coy. W Company to march off at 1-15 p.m.

   Movements East of N. road will be by platoons at 50yd interval.

2. All permanent working parties and schemes of work will be handed over on relief.

3. Taking over lot pistes to be rendered to Battn. H.Q. by Noon 30th inst. Lists of all trench stores to be entered in Coy Books.

4. 7th R.I.R. will hand over Gascrés to 1st R.M.F. these to become trench stores.

5. Completion of relief to be immediately reported to Battn. H.Q. in code by wire.

6. Valises will be stacked at the Guard Hut and packs and 1 blanket per man will be stacked in their company lines ready for removal by Noon.

7. Transport Officer will arrange for Transport.

Issued at:-   J. Crawley Lieut.
28-10-16   A/Adjutant 1st R. Munster Fus.

www.ingramcontent.com/pod-product-compliance
Lightning Source LLC
Chambersburg PA
CBHW081436160426
43193CB00013B/2302